THE DIARY OF
DARREN TACKLE

THE DIARY OF
DARREN TACKLE

as told to
Jim White

WARNER BOOKS

A *Warner* Book

First published in Great Britain in 1998
by Warner Books

A CIP catalogue record for this book
is available from the British Library.

ISBN: 0 7515 2587 1

Typeset by Palimpsest Book Production Limited,
Polmont, Stirlingshire
Printed and bound in Great Britain
by Clays Ltd, St Ives plc

Warner Books
A Division of
Little, Brown and Company (UK)
Brettenham House
Lancaster Place
London WC2E 7EN

To Bols
Top of the league always

ACKNOWLEDGEMENTS

Of course, the first person I should like to thank is Rodney, my agent, who worked out that this book might be a nice little earner for the pair of us. Top man, Rods. Leader in his field.

I'm also very grateful to all my fans, not just at the Daihatsu, but around the country and indeed the whole world who have sustained me during this difficult year. I can tell you, that one letter of support I got from the geezer what wrote in in crayon saying he modelled himself on me really kept me going. Whereabouts is Broadmoor by the way?

And I mustn't forget all the coaches and managers I've played under who helped me with the fundamentals in the game. Specially my first-ever coach, Ted at Flixton St-Germain, who taught me the most important rule about being a modern-day English defender: how to clear it, clear it far and clear it often.

Also, thanks to me team-mates – Wattsy and the lads – what know exactly how to keep up a lad's spirit when it's down. And to Marco, Big Jimmy at Jimini's down River Street, and all the bar staff at the Ferret & Pie Stall for your discretion. And to Nigel, what takes care of everything to do with Tackle Wear.

Last – though only really because I'm contractually obliged – I have to mention Jim White, who helped me with me spelling and that when we were doing the manuscript. And he says he wants to thank Matt, whose idea it was, and Ben who thought up the name, and Cat for sorting things, plus Mike and Rog and everyone else at the *Guardian* who laughed and helped things on.

I love you all. Well, some of you.

Top Shot!

PLAYER QUESTIONNAIRE: DARREN TACKLE

FULL NAME: Darren Tackle.

NICKNAME: The Dog. Or Dazza.

AGE: 25.

POSITION: Wing-back.

MARITAL STATUS: Presently at home to Auntie Palm.

CHILDREN: One, Krystalle (aged four).

BROTHERS OR SISTERS: Lee was an apprentice at Chesterfield, now works as an executive stock facilitator at Shoppalott; Clayton has recently captained the Strangeways football team and at the moment can always help you with a bit of this or that.

FAVOURITE TV PROGRAMME: *Only Fools and Horses*.

FAVOURITE FOOD: Pot Noodle.

FAVOURITE DRINK: Lucozade NRG (hope you're reading this, Boss?!).

THE DIARY OF DARREN TACKLE

FAVOURITE HOLIDAY DESTINATION: Dominican Republic.

FAVOURITE MOVIE: *Goodfellas*. And *Reservoir Dogs*.

FAVOURITE RECORD: *Ocean Drive* by the Lighthouse Family.

LAST BOOK YOU READ: Who do you think I am, Mr Memory?

PETS: Vinnie and Julian, my Staffordshires.

CARS: Jeep Cherokee XRD; BMW M7; Audi A8 (sponsored car provided by Kelner & Kelner, VW & Audi sales, Railway Street – 'Service our speciality').

PERSON YOU WOULD MOST LIKE TO SHARE A ROMANTIC MEAL WITH: Sandra Bullock.

PERSON YOU WOULD LEAST LIKE TO SHARE A LIFT WITH: The Boss (only joking!?).

AMBITION WHEN A YOUNGSTER: To run faster than my brother Clayton.

AMBITION NOW: To be safely retired on a yacht sailing round the Caribbean by the time I'm thirty.

PET HATES: The media and that what don't seem to realise we professionals deserve a bit of privacy in our private lives.

FAVOURITE WAY TO SPEND SUNDAY MORNING: Lazing in bed with a couple of tabloids reading what exploits the other lads have got up to with some lapdancer in a night-club.

BIGGEST INFLUENCE ON YOUR CAREER: Rodney, my agent (Mr 25 Per Cent).

BIGGEST FEAR: Getting dropped.

BEST FEATURE: My tattoo (and I'm not telling you where it is).

WORST FEATURE: The scar left by another tattoo I had took off.

FAVOURITE PLAYER AS A YOUNGSTER: Julian Dicks.

ROLE MODEL: Mark Dennis.

LUXURY YOU'D TAKE TO A DESERT ISLAND: A bird.

GOAL FOR THIS SEASON: Win the Premiership, the FA Cup and the Coca-Cola. Failing that, 37 per cent absolute minimum hike in my contract. Actually, I don't much care about the first bit as long as I gets the second.

INTRODUCTION

You think, don't you, you lot, that it's easy being a professional footballer these days. Specially in the Premiership. Pampered, that's the word you use. You read in the papers about how much we're pulling down and you think we're buried in cash, up to our eyes in wallop, suffocating in sponds. And for what, you say, as you clock on for another long day manning the phones at the 0800 call centre or whatever bollocks you do for a living. You can't understand how we can earn more in a week than you do in a year for buggering around in the fresh air for two hours every morning and a bit of a kickaround once in while, watched by a bunch of Page Three dollies, panting to lick our wounds.

Well let me ask you a question to help put all this in perspective. Do you know what a convertible stock option is? Course you don't. So you've no idea how difficult it is to decide whether to invest in them, or in high-yielding bearer bonds. Yeah, and I bet you think an off-shore trust vehicle is something what pulls a big yellow tyre round off the beach at San Antonio with a couple of squawking Dorises in it, off their faces on that shangri-la, or whatever that Spanish plonk's called. Well, it's not. I can tell you now: an off-shore trust vehicle is summat to do with money.

Now, you see, that's the kind of thing I have to worry

about. I have my financial adviser on the mobile maybe two, three times a week giving me advice about where to invest for the best returns. That is just not the sort of stuff you'll ever have to get your head round. I'm not complaining, I'm just pointing out that wealth, fame and the ability to go into any pub in town and never put your hand in your pocket all night (unless it's a Blue pub, in which case you keep well out) have their down-sides. It's not all sex, drugs and lager-top for Darren Tackle, you know. Well, not for forty-eight hours before a game, anyhow.

Also, don't believe what you read in the papers about how much we're earning. Let's set the record straight, here and now: after tax, stoppages, mortgage payments, insurance, food, clothes, the car, the Jeep, the motorbike, the snooker table, the other car, the account at Coral's, the holidays, the child maintenance and a couple of bob for me mam have been taken into consideration, I don't suppose I've got much more left in a month than a head-master, a chief constable or a senior doctor totals in a year. It is, as Ruud Gullit put it so neatly, all about gross and netto, innit.

But at the end of the day, as I say, my argument is, we earn it. For one reason and one reason only: pressure. I mean, you don't know what pressure is until you've been a professional footballer. Well, not unless you've had a tyre pump from the garage shoved up your arse, then turned up to about 70 pound a square inch you don't.

Here's just one example of the kind of pressure we live under. Think yourself lucky you don't have to stay awake half the night wondering what mark the geezer in the paper has given you for your performance. Yeah, you know who I'm talking about, that bloke at the *People* what only gave me a three for that Coca-Cola tie at the Manor last year. Don't think I don't know who you are and where you live.

See, you lot who work at Shoppalott, you don't have to worry about getting a three for the way you arranged them kiwi fruit and coriander salads on the shelves the other week, do you? And you down at Exorzt-U-Like, you never get marks out of ten for popping a new set of radials on a Ford Orion, do you? Mind you, just as well. If I was giving them out, I tell you, I'd have given you lot a big fat zero for that exhaust you lobbed on me Jeep the other week. I've told your boss, he can send the bleedin' bailiffs round and all, I'm not paying.

Point is, what I'm talking about is pressure. That's what we're paid for. Fair dos, it's passable wedge. I'm not complaining. Though sometimes when I read in the papers how much some pillock like Carlton Palmer's pulling down, it makes my blood boil. But that's just an issue between me, my agent Rodney, and Mr Chairman. Well, us plus a few journalists at a couple of papers who can float a 'Darren Tackle unhappy with present contract' story.

So when I was contacted by Rodney on me mobile saying that some book people wanted to do an in-depth, fly-on-the-jockstrap, no-holds-barred diary of a Premier league player's season, you know, give an insider the chance to tell it like it really is, get past what you hear in the media and that, let you punters know the real story, the pain, the pressure, oh and the laughs too, my first instinct was this: what's in it for me? I mean, Teddy Sheringham, he's just landed 150 long 'uns for his tale, so's John Barnes, and Les Ferdinand didn't get much less for his. And as for Alex 'Fergie' Ferguson, he's just hauled in a million for his yarn. Which works out at about a 50p a whinge, dunnit.

When Rodders told me the figure the book people had in mind, though, I have to say, I was disappointed. I mentioned it to a couple of the other lads in the dressing-room, and they said they'd got at least double that for their autobiographies. And come to think of it, I think I got more for that video I done last year, *Born to Dazzle: The Darren Tackle Story*.

Now, I'm not greedy, but you must appreciate I've only got a limited life at the top. You lot can be working in pyramid selling of household cleansing equipment or whatever till you're well into your fifties. With this game, it'll be all over by the time I'm thirty. Well, hopefully. So I can't sell myself short, otherwise I could still be playing when I'm thirty-six. Which is more than embarrassing, as Rushie, Pearcie, Barnesie and them lot prove.

Anyhow, Rodders said that was the final offer, and I ought to take it, otherwise the book people were going to approach Graeme Le Saux. And, he said, his motto is: a little bit of something is better than sod-all of nothing.

'That's basically it in a nutshell,' he says. 'You've got a choice in this game, go home with sponds or go home with bollocks. Understand what I'm trying to tell yer, boy? We've all got eggs what need boiling. Got to get off the phone now. Speakcha.'

Besides, he says, it's not as if there's much to it. Just a couple of hours on the mobile with some wuss from one of the papers, and the book people'll do the rest. Plus it might raise my media profile, which, to be fair, has been rather low since that unfortunate incident on Central telly's late-night irreverent sports chat show involving Gary Newbon, a fire extinguisher and Big Ron's signet ring.

So here we are, then: *The Diary of Darren Tackle*, the fruit of nine months' hard labour. I've not read it, obviously. But the geezer what I worked with tells me there's plenty in it what will get me talked about. And then he laughed. Funnily enough, I've never had his phone number, he's only ever called me, so I've not had the chance to ask him why. Anyhow: enjoy. And if you don't, so what. I've banked the cheque. Or rather

Rodders has done it for me. No point hiring a monkey and then grinding your own organ, is there?

Darren Tackle
8 August 1998

SEPTEMBER

Wednesday 3rd

Top night last night. Started at the charity opening of a new place down River Street called the Cross Bar. Wasn't going to go, but Rodney, my agent, said it would be good for my image right now to be seen supporting a charity. He says: show you're putting something back into the community, present a caring face and it could be worth at least another couple of long 'uns on your next boot contract.

'Keep us all from Carey Street, boy,' he says. 'Understand me?'

Plus, he says, there'd be a 500 in it – cash. Which always comes in handy if I was to bump into Marco later on.

Minging gaff, as it happens. There was a group of us there: me, Wattsy, Bubbles, plus Vic and Bob. We all got there early: churlish to let the free bar down. I had three bottles of that new Indonesian lager, with Japanese whisky chasers and half a dozen of them cocktails called Manhattan Kneecapping or something which is like half-set jelly but kicks, I tell you. Knock-out. Pity we were only there ten minutes. But you can't stay longer because the punters start mithering. You'd think, as it was for charity, they'd have a bit more respect. But punters can be knob. Take the owner: he gave us right jip when we said we was leaving.

'Oh, but the orphans aren't here yet,' he was going. 'The bloke from the local paper's coming and all. Can't you hang on another five or so?'

Big mistake. Your modern professional hangs on for no man. Wattsy told him he could shove his orphans, we'd been there long enough and anyhow we only deal with the nationals. I thought there was going to be a right row, but the geezer backed down and give each of us an envelope as we left, so we done our bit.

After that we went to Manzi's, Gracelands, McAffery's, the Firkin Barsteward, Bizzy Mz Lizzy's and ended up at Joie de Vivre. Floor to ceiling totty, gagging for it. Can't remember mine's name. Didn't bump into Marco all night, see, so had nothing to sober us up.

Thursday 4th

I take my diet well seriously. As a professional, I appreciate that my body is my tool: I look after it. We had a bloke from the university in during the pre-season to tell us what to eat, all the nutrients and that. So now, for three days leading up to a game, I only eat bananas. High energy, quick delivery. And easily digestible, which is vital for muscle fatigue, or something. Trouble is, that kind of health scran is about as much use for a hangover as Tomas Brolin is at a Weight Watchers convention. So I stop for a fry-up on the way to training.

I've decided, by the way, I'm not taking the new engine (BMW M7 in Jamaican Avocado, since you're asking) in to training. I know it's tasty, but there's that many anoraks mithering around the training ground these days, it's not worth risking it. They all think they deserve a piece of you – last season some arse pulled the wing-mirror off the old Mazda. Then, two days later, he's only back asking me to sign it. Fans: sometimes I reckon the game would be a whole lot better without them.

So I goes in in the Jeep – functional, practical, versatile: makes a statement about the geezer what drives it, I reckon. Just as I'm parking it between Carmine's Ferrari and Hermann's Merc, Old Demo, the assistant manager, comes sprinting over. He says the Boss wants to see me in his office. Pronto.

I reckon it's probably a late call-up from Mick McCarthy to the Ireland squad (Rodders dropped him a note a couple of months ago to tell him my cousin Barry used to be barman in Killarney) and so I run into the office, giving it plenty to Adele, the Boss's secretary. She's the one Wattsy had in the bedding section at last year's HumungoStore Christmas bash, and he said she was a top ride, although there was something a bit strange about her: at the point of coming, he says, she suddenly shouts out Graham Kelly's name.

Anyhow, when I sees the Boss, it's obviously not the emergency call-up to join the Guinness boys. We're all in there – Wattsy, Vic, Bob, me – and he's got his bollocking face on him: puce with grey piping.

'What the fuckenell is fucken this?' he screams, slamming a copy of the local paper on his desk. 'Fuckenell. Eh? Eh? EH?'

Boss-talk. You get used to it.

On the front page is a picture of some spazz lad in a wheelchair, all big-eyed and sad, under the headline: 'ARROGANT SOCCER STARS SPURN CHARITY KIDS'.

'Gaffer, gaffer, gaffer, relax,' says Wattsy. 'The gentlemen and me turned up, showed our faces, done our bit. You know what the media are like. Desperate to blow everything out of proportion.'

'Let fucken me be the fucken judge of fucken that!' he screams, and starts reading from the paper.

'Fuckenell, eh? "Heartbroken Billy Wallsgrove, nine, had his dreams shattered last night when a group of the Greens' top players left a charity function at the newly opened Cross Bar on River Street just before he and seven other wheel-chair-bound orphans arrived from the B&Q Caring for the Community Orphans' home to meet them." Fuckenell, eh? Eh?

'"The Cross Bar manager, Dale Rawding, 28, said, 'The players behaved very arrogantly. They only stayed five minutes, enjoyed our hospitality and then left. It saddens me that as professional sportsmen, idols to youngsters not just in this town but across the country, they were not prepared to set an example. It seemed they were only interested in publicity, not in charity. We are all very disappointed, but nevertheless the Cross is open for business as usual, with the function room available for private parties at very reasonable rates, telephone now for details.'"

'Fuckenell. There's more. "Young Billy was particularly upset that he missed Greens' wing-back Darren Tackle. 'I was after his autograph,' said Billy."'

'Sound kid,' I says.

'"I already have it nine times, but another boy at school was willing to swap ten Darren Tackles for one Tony Cottee."'

Knob.

For some reason, at this, the Boss starts to calm down. You can tell when he's easing after a bate, that little nerve under his eye stops flickering like the oil warning light on a snide Sierra.

'Oh fuckenell, son,' he says. 'What are the shareholders going to fucken, you know, think? There's a bunch of blokes from some pension fund on a fact-finding tour of the catering facilities in the new Alliance & fucken Leicester stand as we speak. Worse, I've got old fucken wossit, you know, Slimey Simon from the local rag what broke the story outside, I'll have to fucken give the fucker summat.'

He stops for a minute, then he drops the big one.

'I've no option, lads, I'll have to fucken fine you all a week's money.'

Double knob.

'Yeah, and you'll donate it to charity.'

Treble knob.

'But,' he says. Then he smiles. 'The charity will be of my choice. And this month the Greens' nominated charity is the players' pool, with ten per cent going into the gaffer's retirement fund. Now get the fucken, you know, fuck out.'

Top man, the Boss. Hard but fair. Earns the respect of his team.

Friday 5th

I've got a new nickname for myself: the Dog. Any pro'll tell you, nicknames is a big part of the game, help forge camaraderie and that. At our place it's a massive part of the laugh you have as a bunch of lads. For a start there's Lee Davies and Nicky Donaldson, who are known as Vic and Bob, so-called after them two off-of that telly programme, *Shooting Stars*, because they stick together and are well mental and that. Then there's the keeper, who's known as Hermann because he's German. Actually he's Norwegian; Tor-Blimey Liefitoutson or something, that's his real name, but he looks like a Kraut, so he's Hermann. Oh, and Mickey Jackson, he's known as Bubbles. I know what you're thinking: Michael Jackson's his name and the real Michael Jackson's got a pet chimp called Bubbles. But no, it's cleverer than that. He's called Bubbles because he likes to let one go in the team bath. Sharp, eh?

With most of the lads you just shorten the name. Like Gary Ball, who's known as Bally or Bollocks or Balls, because it's shorter. Well, it's not, it's longer, but you know what I mean: vital for communication on the park, really. Yours truly is known as Dazz, Dazza or sometimes Tacky. Which I'm thinking is a bit unimaginative. Hence: the Dog.

I tried it out in training this morning, you know, subtle-like, see if any of the lads'd pick up on it.

'Dog's ball,' I shouts when making a clearing header. And 'Dog's in space' when over-lapping in the five-a-sides. When someone wants the ball, I tells them no point asking for it unless you ask right. From now on, I only respond to the Dog.

It doesn't take Wattsy long to notice. He comes up to me and says: 'May I ask a practical question at this juncture? What's all this Dog bollocks?'

And I says: 'That's it.'

'What is?'

'Dog, as in the dog's bollocks. As in Darren Tackle is the dog's bollocks. As in coolest geezer in the club. So from now on I wish to be addressed only as Dog.'

'Dog. I see, that's about right,' says Wattsy. 'Because you, Darren, are about as cool as a dog's arse what's just shat.'

Bollocks training session all round, as it happens. Old Demo, the assistant manager (so named because he's a right sadist like that Demon Headmaster off-of kid's telly), he's got a new routine he nicked from watching Cuban baseball players prepare. Improve our spatial awareness, or something, he reckons. All I know was, it was lots of bending and twisting. Christ it hurt. We all complained: can't we just stick with five-a-sides?

Afterwards, felt so crap I couldn't face doing an interview Rodney had arranged with some new football magazine. I could see the geezer hanging around out front, so I got a YTS kid to tell him I'm not here. Geezer complains he's come all the way from London and it's been arranged for months, there's a studio booked for the photo-shoot and the clothes have got to go back to Italy tomorrow, but the kid just hassles him away. Nice one. I'll tell Rodders I thought it was next week and go home for a kip. As a pro I take my responsibilities seriously, you've got to these days, and what I need right now is quality rest.

Wednesday 17th

Last night's first game in the Coca-Cola has taken its toll. A bloody joke: that's quite literally the only way to describe it. That or a barrel of shite. We were drawn against that Neanderthal bunch of third-division shin saboteurs from up the ring-road. A real David against Goliath battle, the *Mirror* called it. Except, even at our school, they never taught us that David won that particular local derby by wrapping his studs round Goliath's cruciates, did they?

It was a kick-fest. Wall-to-wall bruise construction. Kind of game that makes you wonder why you bother.

Seriously, it worries me the consequences of the growing gap between the rich and the poor in football these days. Like the bitterness: all these lads trying to take it out on us just because we're on ten grand a week, are decked out head-to-toe in designer clobber and drive top-of-the-range German while the best they can manage is a once-a-month scour of their local Woodhouse and a preferential personal loan on a sponsor's Vauxhall Vectra.

So as a consequence of them being fired up on rocket-fuel levels of envy, we're kicked out of the Coca-Cola at the first attempt. An embarrassing fiasco, made all the worse by the fact we stepped out in our new one-off limited-edition kit for use in Coca-Cola cup, aways only.

Now, like everyone else, I'd been made up over the summer when Mr Chairman said he was going to get in a designer to do our new outfit. About time too. After all, Norwich had Bruce Oldfield to do theirs, even Orient got Jasper Conran in; it should have been a case of out with the Umbro, in with the Uomo Vogue. A book was even opened in the dressing-room predicting who we'd get. Bob had a pony on Alexander McQueen; Vic had a monkey on Gianni Versace (not a big paper reader, Vic); me I put a long 'un on Stella McCartney.

But, typically, Mr Chairman took a short-cut and got some student in from the design college. Seeking to redefine sporting apparel as a leading-edge fashion statement is what she said she was doing. Making us look like a bunch of tossers is what she did.

I'll quote from the merchandise catalogue: 'Cut a dash in our new limited-edition Coca-Cola away kit, tailored in E-Z-Breeth™, the revolutionary new two-way stretch dralon fabric. Fashioned in aubergine and strawberry, with magenta inlay jacquering, it comes complete with tapered torso, flared sleeves and, in an homage to the now-departed poet laureate of football, a pre-starched, permanently erect collar.'

Yeah, and has the wassock what wrote that tried playing in it? At half-time we told the Boss he had to make a change, it was too embarrassing. We told him to do a Fergie and tell the press it was because we couldn't see each other. Mind you, fat chance in that arrangement. But he went mental. Fuckenell this and fuckenell that. Had we no respect for the efforts of the people who made this club what it is today, he says, i.e. the commercial department.

'We need to sell this kit to pay you lots' fucken

inflated wages. Now get out there and stop fucken whin-ing.'

No wonder we were blasted out.

My evening ended on a right downer. All night I get kicked up the arse, kicked in the shin and kicked where I've just been kicked. And then, when I was making me way off after we've lost, I get a couple of yonners in their end screaming as how they're going to report me to the dibble for clearing me nose as I pass them. Tossers: as if I'd waste it. Amount I'm spending with Marco at the moment I could flog my snot at 50 quid a G.

Monday 22nd

It's like the United Nations at our gaff these days. Over the summer the Boss acquired three Bosnians, an Azerbaijani and a lad with four caps for the breakaway republic of Chechnya.

Now I'm all for the foreign invasion, provided they're prepared to integrate, do things our way, you know, show they mean business. Like Darko, for instance, who's assimilated himself into the local way of life totally, even did a three-month stretch in the middle of last season for fencing stolen car parts.

But this latest wave of continentals at our place seem determined to bring along their own customs. They're almost deliberately trying not to fit in, and are thus undermining the whole dressing-room morale. For a start, there's the Bosnians staying back in the afternoons for extra workouts in the gym. Then it turns out the Azerbaijani never has more than a glass of red wine with his pasta. And to cap it all, this Chechen bloke, he's only gone and revealed he's a vegetarian.

But the worst of the lot is Carmine, our Paraguayan

midfield maestro as they call him in the posh papers, who has been wanting away all summer, but as no one's come in for him, is still here. Let me tell you one thing that sums up this Carmine: he's the only geezer in the club what never gets called by a nickname. Basically this is a bloke who does not want to be one of the lads, despite all our best efforts to involve him.

Take today, before our appearance on the Monday Night Match what is being televised live on Sky. As I say, what a laugh we have in our dressing-room. What Bob done before the game, I tell you, I was doubled up. Carmine, right, gets all this stuff before matches brought in from all his girlie fans. Some of what he gets you would not believe. Because he's foreign and that, he chucks it in the bin. But Wattsy's fished it out a couple of times and it's well saucy, girlies telling Carmine what they want to do to him. Wattsy took some of it home with him once last season, said he wanted to study it in private.

As it happens, he's got a bit of a reputation as a swordsman, Carmine. First night he was in town, he went out larging it down River Street, and copped for this right pair of Dorises, all top knots, Wonderbras and the kind of eyes that can size up a lad's wallet at fifty paces. Next day, they sold their story to the *Mirror*. Though he's getting to grips with it now, when he first arrived a year or so back, he was well dodgy in the English department, and according to the story in the paper he'd picked them up by using his pocket translating machine. They'd spotted him in a bar and gone up to him, and he'd keyed in a couple of words into his machine and shown it to them. And the words were: 'hotel', 'room' and 'now'.

'Eee, but they're so Romantic, these Latins,' one of the slappers told the paper. 'And he never needs any of that Niagra or whatever it was called. I tell you, he was up all night.'

That's Carmine: fanny magnet. But poseur. We reckon

he needed taking down a notch or two. So Bob, he pops one of his special parcels on the bench under the geezer's peg in the dressing-room before the game, all nicely wrapped up with a fancy label and that. Carmine's about to chuck it like he always does, but Vic gives it: 'No, Carmine, mate, some bird's gone to a lot of trouble, open it, mate.'

So the geezer does. And what's inside? Bob's only gone and laid a great steaming Richard the Third in a shoe box, hasn't he.

This is the standard Bob dressing-room joke. He has a thing about turds. One thing he likes doing is, while you're having a pre-match dump in the dressing-room bogs, he'll slip a turd on a piece of newspaper under the door and suddenly jerk the paper out from under it, so you're sitting there, shorts down, a Richard between your ankles, knowing you can't move. Not for nothing does our Bob have a reputation as a footballing wit.

Anyhow, Carmine, the moment he spots what's going on, goes mental. He takes a swing at Bob, misses, trips and ends up stepping in the Richard in his new Patrick Cox loafers. Course, we're all killing ourselves, but he storms right out. As Grandad (real name Mickey Scanlan, so named because he's an embarrassment still playing at 33) says: 'Welcome to England, son.' He may be so old he's close to senile, Grandad, but he's right: these foreign lads, they've got to learn that a sense of humour's vital in our game.

Tuesday 23rd

Papers are full of the Boss's little tirade on Sky last night. He blew his top with George Gavin in the post-match interview in front of the sponsors' board. Nothing to do with us losing the third on the bounce, he's getting quite used to that. No, it was when Gavin asked about why Carmine suddenly pulled out of the game that the Boss starts ranting. Fuckenell this, fuckenell that, about how everyone on Sky's a secret Blue, out to do us down. When he's in that kind of mood, every bit of crockery within a twenty-mile radius goes into hiding.

What with everything else that's going on, Wattsy decides to call a team meeting for tonight. Now these are a vital component of our team spirit. Every so often, we get together as a bunch of lads and iron out the problems facing us all. Find out who the strong lads are, find out who you can trust when the chips are down and that. Usually they take place at Mad Mick O'Shea's pub by the station. Nice and quiet, unobtrusive, perfect place to iron out a few problems, you know, collectively assume responsibility and all that.

But tonight, Wattsy suggests we try that place up by the airport, Dell's it's called. Top totty action, up there. But not your Carmine-style Doris. Up at Dell's you're talking carpeted in style: models, divorcees, bored rich housewives keen on a helping hand from the manual labouring classes.

Sensing the kind of evening that lies ahead, I've put on me new Comme des Garçons top, new Issey Miyake jeans and new Gucci suedes in a dazzling shade of lilac. Add in me Tommy Hilfiger import-only trunks, total cost of outfit: £1,150. Fortnight's wages for your average third-division nonce.

What with all the points we're picking up at the moment (on licences, not in the league), Wattsy decided it was best for us to get a cab, which calls for us all one by one. The first bad sign of the evening is, when we get to Dell's, I lose a quick round of paper, stone, scissors, so I end up picking up the fare. As I'm paying the geezer the others have all piled into the club. I'm about to run through – head down, don't want the punters spotting you, see – when the bouncer stops me and says: 'Sorry, sir, no jeans.'

I says, 'You're kidding, these are Issey Miyake, have you any idea how much they cost?'

And he says: 'Sorry, that's the rule: Tuesday night is pants night.'

So I goes mental and give it the old do-you-know-who-I-am routine. He says he knows very well who I am. Knobber: he's obviously a Blue.

I have to ring up me stepdad, Donald, on the mobile and tell him to get up there pronto with a pair of strides. He was well cheesed-off, but I know him: he'll do anything for a tenner. I'm standing outside the place for twenty minutes, clocked by loads of punters, before he arrives. He just chucks the trousers out the car window, demands his money and drives off. There's nowhere to change so I just do it there and then, in the car-park.

Then, just as I'm getting out of me Issey's, some punter goes past, says, 'Ooh look, that's Tacky,' gets her Instamatic out and takes a snap. Unreal: they just think they own you.

And then after all that, as I'm going in, the bouncer says: 'Sorry, sir, didn't I tell you, it's jacket night tonight.'

That's it. I get a cab home. On the way back, the mobile rings: it's the lads, it was all a wind-up, they say; they'd paid the bouncer a fifty to stop me getting in. He'll let me in now if I head back, they say. No way. It's pathetic. You wonder when some people are going to grow up.

Friday 26th

Get into training and there they all are, gathered round the *Sun*, smirking. 'What's up?' I says.

'What's up, Dog?' says Wattsy. 'Have a butcher's at that, Snoop Doggy Dog Breath.'

He chucks me the paper and on the back page is a picture of me, with me jeans round me ankles in the car-park at Dell's under the headline: 'WORLD EXCLUSIVE. SOCCER SHOCKER: DARREN SHOWS HIS TACKLE'. I tell you, sense of humour or no sense of humour, I'm going to bloody kill them.

OCTOBER

Monday 6th

Crap week. With the internationals coming up, and most of the other lads off to join their squads, I'm one of the stiffs left behind. Trouble is, Hoddle just doesn't fancy me for his system. It's all Graeme Le Saux, Gareth Southgate and anyone what's worn a Man U. shirt. As a professional, obviously, I'm prepared to keep quietly plugging away, let me performances speak for themselves, and hopefully one day I'll achieve the pinnacle of any pro's career and represent my country.

But if he doesn't pick me soon, I'll be looking for pastures new. Another country. And that's not blackmail – Darren Tackle is not one to issue idle threats. That's just plain fact. I'll give 110 per cent for anyone's cause, motivated solely by professional pride. Well, that and the extra few noughts an international cap puts on your bottom line.

As yet, though, the old Northern Ireland granny scam isn't working. The geezer from the Irish FA rang last week to say he's researched it and apparently my old nan came from Hartlepool. Looks like I'll have to get Rodders to drop a line to the Jocks about me Uncle Angus, then.

The other thing that's cheesing me off about this week already is that sometimes during international lay-offs, the Boss takes us left-overs on a bit of sun to Playa de las Americas or Tenerife or somewhere for the free weekend. Nice stroll, few relaxing beers, bubble in the jacuzzi, chance to unwind with the lads. But none of that this week. Oh no, we've been left back here to rust in the rain while he's busy in South America trying to persuade Carmine to come back.

Carmine, right, has caught the first plane home after that stroke Bob pulled on him. The papers are loving it. First thing Carmine does when he gets to Bogotá or wherever, is get on the blower whingeing about how we English don't train properly, don't eat properly, booze too much, generally aren't professional in our preparation and how he's had to get the hell out to get back into a proper routine and put himself in the frame for Paraguay's World Cup squad. He's got to remember his priorities, he says. Who pays his wages and that. Which is odd, because I thought our lot paid them.

Course, the papers haven't a clue what's really going on, so they buy it hook, line and stinker, with all the pundits going on about a clash of cultures and the posh papers lining up to say this is just typical of the decline of English football. Which shows what they know: it was all about a turd in a box. So, sniffing controversy, now the *Sun*, the *Mirror* and the *Mail* have all got reporters out there, camped outside his mam's house, coming up with these long stories about his impoverished childhood and how him and his seven brothers used to play on the barrios with nothing to kick around but of a bunch of old rags.

It makes me laugh this love affair the papers have got with foreigners. As if me and our Lee and our Clayton didn't used to be on the rec behind our house all hours when I was a kid, with nothing, as I recall, to kick around except a World Cup 1986 placky ball from Woolies our dad brought us on one of his rare visits. I were always Bryan Robson: I'd got that fall clutching at your dislocated shoulder down to a tee. We was out there every minute of the day. That was till I was fourteen, when the School of Excellence banned me from kickarounds for insurance reasons. Come to think of it, though, it may have been before that. It was probably until our Clayton had to go away to that school everyone reckoned was good. You know, the one they approved of.

Anyway, I reckon good riddance to Carmine: yeah, sure, he can chip a keeper from fifty yards and play keepy-uppy with a golf ball for three days while balancing half a dozen beer bottles across his shoulders, but if the geezer can't take a joke, he's going to undermine the whole dressing-room. Morale will plummet. It's a fact of nature, as sure as Ginger Spice's tits'll soon be sagging. Well, not quite, 'cos nobody's yet found a way to inject silicone into morale. The Boss, though, can't see it with Carmine. He's so far up the geezer's arse he needs an aqualung.

One good thing about the lay-off weekend, it means some of the injuries we've been picking up will have a chance to sort themselves. We've had a spate lately: Bob twisted an ankle leaving the bookie's, one of the two Bosnians the Boss bought over the summer has gone down with gut-rot after breaking into the McDonald's family stand and overdosing on chocolate milkshake, and Wattsy's on the bench for a month after bashing his nose against the bathroom mirror. It was lying on his coffee table at the time.

Tuesday 7th

Training's not going well. Old Demo reckons the break's a good chance to get us up to speed. He says we're not sharp enough, that's why we've lost the last three on the bounce, so it's circuits, circuits, circuits. It's only after

I've done seven that I realise I'm the only one there. Me and a couple of YTS no-hopers. There's not a solid first-team geezer in sight. Not one.

When I gets back in the dressing-room, after Old Demo's supervised 200 press-ups in the slush in the centre circle, there's not a sign of anyone in there either. I try every room: the solarium, the sauna, the video lounge, the bar (ours is a new training complex, Lottery-funded, and full of the kind of hi-tech equipment needed to get an athlete into the peak of physical condition). Not a sniff. Then I try the physio room. They're all in there, everyone of them not on international call, warm as toast: Wattsy, Vic, Bob, even Old Grandad, all prevailing themselves of the services of Suzette, the new physio recruited from Toulouse rugby club over the summer.

When I walk in, there's a few piss-taking cheers.

'What you doing, Dazza?' says Vic. 'We seen you wasting all that energy out training. What you want to do is get yourself a little knock, son, and join the real men under the fingers of the lovely Suzette here.'

Turns out the lot of them have reported in with little niggles, pulled hammies, chest cold, that sort of thing, excusing themselves from training.

'Don't you know that as a professional, Dazz, you've got to save yourself for the big games?' says Bob, pulling tight the belt on his terry towelling robe with the club crest embossed on the chest.

'Very true, Robert,' chips in Wattsy. 'Though some might say, the way Dog End here has been playing recently, he's been saving himself *during* the big games.'

Ha bloody ha. Frankly, I'm beginning to see what Carmine's on about.

Friday 10th

After a morning in the queue at the physio's, I'm down to a studio in the Quays for a photo-shoot Rodney fixed up. When your career's as short as a professional footballer's you've got to plan for the future, and I reckon I fancy doing a bit of modelling when I've finished. You know, something worthwhile, give something back to the game. Also there's the freebies. Wattsy's done a bit and says it's always good for a new suit or two. I fancy a Cerutti, in midnight blue with five-button front and two vents at the back. Or maybe a Donna Karan, double-breasted, single vent with a light chalk-stripe.

'Basically, boy, all you've got to do is wossname, stand there and that's it in a nutshell,' Rodney says when he bells us on the mobile. 'And make sure you gets the cheque before you leave, boy. Cuts down on administration. Gotta dash, got a couple of eggs what need boiling. Speakcha.'

Anyway, I walks into this studio, past a tidy bit of skirt on reception it has to be said, and it's just nylon crap piled up everywhere. I says, where's the suits? And the photographer, who right fancies himself, says, 'Didn't Rodders tell you? This is a shoot for the special Christmas edition of the club's merchandise catalogue. You're the only face who'll do it.'

So instead of a Nicole Farhi jacket, I'm in a 'Come On You Mighty Greens' T-shirt and a pair of oven gloves embroidered with cartoon pictures of Carmine's cartwheel goal celebration. Then the wuss gets me into some green-striped pyjamas and makes me stand next to Fi-Fi the Flounder, our new cuddly club mascot. She's that seven-foot haddock in a ra-ra skirt with big red lips and ten-inch long fluttery eye-lashes who prats around the touchline before matches, trying to get the River Street End to sing for a bloody change. Anyhow, the wuss snapper geezer wants us to get all intimate, and makes me sit on Fi-Fi's lap. She's got her fins round me and we're puckering up, I'm thinking, never let an opportunity pass, so while the photographer geezer's reloading the camera, I ask for her phone number. It only turns out to be a bloke in there. And worse, he gives me it.

Tuesday 14th

As I say, endorsements, photo-shoots, that kind of thing, it's part and parcel of the game these days. As professionals we just knuckle down and get on with them, obviously we don't let them interfere with anything except our bank accounts. But I am getting significantly naused off about one endorsement I've got and to be honest it's starting to affect me out there where it matters: on the park. That's me boot deal.

Oh, it all started very promisingly. I was well chuffed with the Ultima Tackles. They was state of the art, fashioned in environmentally cured emu-skin, with a trillium carbide sole with an integrated blade stud system for better torsion control. When I first put the prototypes on, I have to admit I was worried they was going to pinch a bit around the final third, but Les, the kit-man, is a demon with the old boot-black and Tipp-Ex, and he said for a twenty it would be no problem decking out me trusty old Puma Kings to look the part.

But the best feature of the boot was the ad on the telly. It had me in all moody soft focus, getting stripped up in this weird psychedelic changing-room, with steam coming out of these industrial pipes everywhere. It looked a bit like that rave club over by the university where Grandad goes every Tuesday for the student night.

Then, the action switches to the away dressing-room, where there's all the oppo crapping themselves. Then it flicks back to me, and I smile, well-hard, as I slip on our new third strip shirt, the one tastefully designed to look sharp with jeans. Then it goes back to the oppo and they're all kneeling in front of this priest getting themselves blessed and there's this altar boy wafting incense around and a couple of them are crying. Then it's back to me, turning up me collar *à la* Eric. Then, the camera pans to me boots and up comes the line: 'Tackle Your Deepest Fears.'

Sound stuff.

Until Vic pipes up at training the day after it was first shown on Sky Sports 3 in that well prestigious slot between *The Footballers' Football Show* and the American wrestling, saying that I didn't exactly look intimidating in a pair of yellow boots. I said they wasn't yellow actually, Victor, they're Andalucian Lemon. Bob says, yeah, lemon boots for a right lemon.

I didn't rise to it, but straight after training I'm on the mobile to Nigel, the boot rep, to see if he can get me a black pair for the following Saturday.

'I think you'll find, Darren,' says this Nigel, 'that para- graph six sub-section three of your contract, as signed by your representative Mr Rodney Gee, indicates that you are obliged to wear the lemon style for three months to tie in with a nationwide above-the-line promotional cam- paign, which also includes five interviews with broadsheet newspapers, two with *FHM* and *Loaded* magazines, plus one public appearance at the city-centre sports shops in the company of Ms Sharron Davies . . .'

Nice one.

'. . . and three other PAs accompanied by Fi-Fi the Flounder.'

And what then?

'Thereafter you will wear the Provençal Lavendar for

three months, before switching, for the run-in at the end of the season, to the Caribbean Sunset Flame.'

Thursday 16th

Get a call on the mobile on the way into training from this geezer Bill I've done a few bits and bobs with from the *People*.

'What do you reckon?' is what he says.

Well, not one to be easily caught out, I've got me endorsement head on straight away and I tell him that I reckon at £149.99, a pair of Ultima Tackles will help any parent satisfy their child's ambitions to play just like the stars.

He says: 'Not your bloody boots, Dazz, I mean about Carmine.'

What about Carmine?

'He's coming back. We've heard the Boss has had to promise him all sorts: own personal trainer, personal chef, three bodyguards, accommodation for his mother, sister and seven brothers to come and live over here with him, plus a cool forty-five grand a week.'

I've almost driven off the road: forty-five a week? What with fines and that at the moment, I reckon I'm lucky to pull that sort of money down in a month.

'Dazz, son, are you there?' the *People* geezer goes. 'Have you any comment to make?'

'If that's the figure he's on, then good luck to him,' I says, just about keeping a discreet lid on it. 'We never discuss wages in our dressing-room. It's a happy ship at the Daihatsu Stadium and Darren Tackle is certainly not the person to start rocking it.'

'A grand help you start it gently swaying?'

'Fifteen hundred.'

'Twelve's me final offer.'

'Call it cash and I'll make the *Titanic* seem like an accident in a boating lake.'

After we've finished the interview, I'm straight on the blower to Wattsy. He says not to worry. There may be the money, the interpreter for Saturday nights down River Street, the club picking up every expense down to the milk bill. But he's heard the accommodation the club's got lined up for the family is that bloody great house up by the airport what Mr Chairman's dodgy building firm built about four years ago what he can never sell.

Now that news has cheered me up no end.

See, I've had some of Mr Chairman's building techniques. Last year, I gets called into his office after training. I thought: la-di-da, Kenny Dalglish has been on the blower, the big time beckons for yours truly.

I'd not been up there before, but what a gaff: the bloody desk alone was the size of the Dell. And it needs to be big because this is the very desk, so Wattsy tells me, over which Mr Chairman has his secretary every Thursday night.

'I won't mess about, son,' Mr Chairman says. 'You know me. Yorkshireman and proud of it. Don't beat about the bush, say what I mean and mean what I say. What's on me lung's on me tongue.'

And I'm sitting there, checking out his woodwork for stains, thinking, well it's got to be Newcastle innit. Or Liverpool at the very least.

'Now, let me tell you why you're here, son,' he says, and I'm thinking, here we go: St James's it is. 'I hear you're looking for somewhere to store your snooker table.'

'So what's that got to do with Kenny Dalglish?' I says.

'Sod-all,' he says, looking at me like I'm pissed. 'Unless he's a dab hand with a cue. Fact of the matter is, I might well be able to do you a tidy little deal on a conservatory.'

'A what?'

'Conservatory. Glass thing. Put up outside your bloody house and pop your table in it. I got a job lot last month, bankrupt stock. Seeing as how it's you, I'll knock a fiver off the brochure price.'

Sound deal, I thought.

Anyhow, it took six months to build, and when it was finished the workmen had to shave six inches off either side the table to get it in. Plus, there was this big gap between the glass and the back wall of me house. When I complained, Mr Chairman told me not to worry, it was for ventilation and by the way, could I pose for some publicity shots for the local paper, standing next to the completed conservatory. So I did.

I got burgled the night after the pictures appeared, and worse, the first time it rained I had the only snooker table in town what needed drainage.

And now Carmine's moved his entire family into that house Mr Chairman built what looks like a public toilet up by the airport.

Warms the cockles, eh.

Saturday 18th

I'm not surprised Carmine's back, though. Once you've played at the top level over here, where else can you go? I tell you where, there's only one place to go: downtown. I mean South American football, it simply can't beat ours for passion and sheer spectator involvement, can it? Just to trot out on to the pitch at the Daihatsu and sample the atmosphere seeping down from the Platinum Club members as they shuffle from the hospitality suites to their seats in the Alliance & Leicester Stand, you can't buy that. As Wattsy says, you could hear a pin drop at our place these days.

Mind you, things got a bit noisy fifteen minutes into today's game when I got sent off for 'raising my arms in an aggressive manner'. I couldn't believe it: quarter of an hour gone and the ref makes a right bollocks of himself.

As Alex Ferguson has said, when these guys look at the telly replays afterwards they really are going to be ashamed of their decisions. No question about it in my case. I recorded *Match of the Day* and even Alan Hansen could see what was going on.

It doesn't take a GCSE in lip-reading to see their winger calling me a right wuss. Then you can see me squaring up and asking him what he's on about. Then, clear as day to everyone except, it seems, the jerkwad in black, you can see him saying only a wuss would wear a pair of lemons on his feet. Seems to me, instead of being sent off, I should have won a community service award for smacking a prat in a public place. But no, as it's me and I'm a marked man as far as refs are concerned, I get redded.

And I tell you what, I could have done without Fi-Fi the Flounder coming up to me as I'm on me way off and giving me a big consolation hug and all.

Anyhow, when I'm in the changing-room running the early bath, I check out the mobile and there's only a message on it from Glenn Hoddle, saying how he's up in the Alliance & Leicester and how he's just witnessed my sending off. So I'm thinking: shite, Wales it is then. But he goes on about how he'll need that kind of fighting spirit in the World Cup and how he was well alarmed to hear I was considering an international career with the Welsh and would it help change my mind if he said he was prepared to guarantee me, here and now, a slot in his World Cup squad?

Now, Darren Tackle is nothing if not broad-shouldered. Obviously I am more than willing to explore the possibility of reconciliation. So I'm straight on the blower, ringing back the number he's left. It's only after Hoddle's droned on about the problems of French food and how he knows it can't be easy committing yourself to a team whose away shirt looks as if it was designed by a room full of gorillas attempting the *Times* crossword and asked me if it would affect my decision to know he had it in mind for the Dog to share a kennel with Gazza, that I clock it's not him at all. It's Wattsy, on the bench, wetting himself.

According to that movie *Goodfellas* (my all-time favourite after *Reservoir Dogs*, as it happens), revenge is a dish best eaten cold. I tell you: I'm just taking mine out the oven.

Wednesday 22nd

After hearing what Carmine's pulling down, I got on to Rodders and told him to land me something worthwhile. On the way in to training he calls on the mobile to tell me he's got me a slot on the Barney Butcher phone-in show.

'The big time beckons, boy,' he says. 'Get the gas on. We are boiling eggs.'

I ask him what the story is dosh-wise, and he says – can you believe it – £85. I says forget it. Darren Tackle is not seen climbing out of his bed for less than a monkey. He says you've got to think of it long-term, the exposure for a media career and that, and what's more they'll send a cab round to pick me up.

In the end I was swung round, mainly because that Barney Butcher's brilliant when he slags everyone off – brilliant. No one's safe, he'll have a pop at anyone, Barney. That one was a belter he told the other week about Stan Collymore being so lazy he's undergoing treatment by the club doctor for bed sores. Besides, if I go on the show, I can have a word with him about slagging us recently: it was well out of order.

Anyhow I do the show and we start off with a chat about the Premiership, who's going to win what, who's got the best foreigner, usual stuff. To be honest, he goes on a bit and I'm getting a little bored. I came on the programme because I know Barney's reputation and thought he'd ask me about me private life and that, which supermodel I fancied, who's the lad in the dressing-room with the best line in cutting-the-toes-off-socks japery, that kind of malarkey. And here he was asking me about the merits of the Christmas tree formation. I mean, it's not on.

Things aren't getting a lot better when he asks me about referees.

'Don't you think, Dazz,' he says, 'that when a ref what makes a rick that affects our side, destroys our season with one peep on his whistle, that we fans, those of us who have laboured long and spent our hard-earned on a place in the cheap seats, should go round forthwith to the geezer's house and smash his windows?'

I laughed.

'No, I mean it. I jest not,' he says. 'Throw me a bone here, Dazz, help me out on this one. Is this not just the thing that will concentrate the minds of those petty Hitlers, those trumped-up little kaisers in black, determined once and for all to ruin this game that you and I love? Address an expectant nation on this topic, Darren. Climb aboard that soap-box. Unburden yourself of the foaming torrent of opinion.'

Well, obviously I'm not falling for that one, I've been on one of the Boss's media-training courses where they warn you about Motty and sly journalists' questions. I remember what Vinnie Jones had to fork out for that disrepute case involving his video *Soccer's Hard Men* which, by some bizarre over-sight did not include any footage of yours truly. So I'm well careful.

'What you got to remember,' I says, 'is that refs are only human, they make mistakes like the rest of us. But their decision on the pitch is final and if you're a professional you just have to grit your teeth and get on with it. Fact of life.'

He doesn't seem happy with that answer.

'Darren, Darren, Darren,' he goes. 'Am I hearing right? Are my ears performing as the Deity intended? You are telling me that these sub-humans, these *untermensch* who have the dazzling chutzpah to refer to themselves as arbiters of the laws of the game come from the same species as you or indeed me? What about the bloke who sent you off last week? His dog could have seen he had made a catastrophic error. His white stick probably saw it. So, tell me, Darren. Cast aside discretion. Worry not about disrepute. Since it should be the FA themselves who are in disrepute allowing that man to officiate gladiatorial engagements involving athletes of the pedigree of your good self. You're among friends now, Darren. Tell me, tell us, tell your people, what do you really think of him?'

So I tell him.

Afterwards Butcher said it made such a change to hear a footballer really speak his mind. He says it made great radio, particularly the bit about putting the ref's bollocks on display in the club museum and charging punters a fiver to see them. And the producer said it was brilliant, they'd never taken calls in the studio from Mr Chairman before. Or Graham Kelly for that matter. Neither wanted to go on air, apparently, they just wanted to tell me they'd be having a word with me when I got home. Quiet nod of congratulation on a new career departure, I expect.

NOVEMBER

Monday 3rd

This was lying on the fax machine this morning:

FROM THE OFFICE OF RODNEY GEE,
FOOTBALL PROMOTIONS LTD.

'Putting the showbiz into soccer'

Audit for Darren Tackle Inc, off-field activities for
the month of October.
Appearance on the Barney Butcher phone-in show.
Fee received: £85.
Less agent's commission @ 25%: £21.25.
Less VAT @ 17.5% on agent's commission: £3.71.
Net now due to Darren Tackle Inc: £60.04.
Fines concurrent on above appearance: £12,000.

So now I know the final cost of free speech. I got back
after that Barney Butcher show a week ago to find my
ansafone lighting up like a dibble's breathalyser when
Wattsy's been driving home from a spot of R & R.
They was all there on it: lawyers, officials, the Boss, Mr
Chairman. Basically all of them wanting to jump straight
down my throat.

It got worse. The hearing at the FA was a farce. No other
word for it. For starters, Rodney's only gone and tipped off
the whole of the media and that about the time and place,

so when we arrive at Lancaster Gate it's pavement to pavement snappers out there. I mean, he could've warned me. I'm only wearing the club blazer, in't I. Complete with a pair of your sensible, impress-the-authorities grey slacks. Thus is me cred dealt an embarrassing blow well below the water line, with pictures of me all over the papers, threaded up like Prince Charles. Then Rodders does an impromptu press conference on the steps as we're walking in.

'I'm distraught that my client is being victimised in this way by a bunch of corrupt officials who wouldn't know a football if it hit them in the face,' he says. 'I'm gutted. I'm kippered. This is my boy. I made him, brung him up with me bare hands. And now this. Even my old colleague Mad Frankie Fraser has never been treated as badly as this. Has the whole world gone mad?'

Always displayed good timing, Rods.

Leaving the jackals behind, we walks into the FA to find Mr Chairman and the Boss already in there. We're all sitting in reception, looking at the wood panelling and the cabinet displaying all the many trophies English football's picked up over the years (the particularly impressive fourth-place shield for the U-15s Girls' British Championship taking pride of place) and I get the sense from the total lack of conversation that I might be on my own in there. Which is roughly how it turns out.

We get led into this upstairs room and the lot of them in there have obviously been watching back episodes of *Rumpole of the Bailey* on UK Gold. They're full of bollocks, pretending it's a court and putting me in the dock and giving me a Bible to swear over (I should've said you needn't have bothered: I can manage quite well without, thanks very much). And they're going on and bloody on about letting the good name of the game down and how players should be setting an example and how youngsters look up to individuals like me. You would think I'd done something really wrong, you know like wilfully wearing a moustache on a football field or releasing a record like that last Man U. effort. All I done was suggest one or two of our leading officials would benefit from testicular surgery without the benefit of anaesthetic and suddenly I'm public enemy number bleedin' one. Christ, it was just a bit of air-wave verbals. Haven't these wusses got no sense of humour?

Obviously not. They slam me with a six G. fine, which the club – in a friendly gesture of solidarity – doubles two days later after the Boss reads some article in the *Sun* accusing him of being soft on discipline, what with the Carmine situation and all.

'You fucken fucker fucken fucked it this time,' is his considered reading of the situation. 'Eh? Eh? Fuckenell.'

After the hearing, as we fights our way through the pack of scum into a taxi, Rodders – never one to exaggerate – calls the decision 'quite frankly the biggest miscarriage of justice since the Birmingham Six' (am I wrong or is that summat to do with Trevor Francis?).

'What is occuring in this country?' he says. 'I'm so naused I have nothing further to say. That's basically all you're getting, boys. That's it in a nutshell. Sod all. Like what we got in there. All right, since you're asking, all I'll say is it's a sad day when the character of the game is being squeezed out by drones in blazers.'

And I'm only standing next to him in a blazer. Knob it.

My humour is not improved by the bleedin' taxi driver telling us how he specialises in hanging around Lancaster Gate, waiting for players after disciplinary hearings. He's had them all in the back of his cab: Norman Hunter, Billy Bremner, Vinnie Jones, Gary Lineker.

'They think the world owes them a living, these footballers,' he says. 'Cut off their bollocks, that would do them the world of good.'

As if I hadn't had it up to here with genitalia. Still, geezer's obviously had some. He told us he picked up Dennis Wise outside the FA once. Which was a bit of a mistake.

Tuesday 4th

So that was a week ago. We're going to appeal, obviously. I mean something's got to give. Since the hearing, there's been two television news crews camped outside me house, plus seven reporters and nine photographers. All of them badgering me, trying to get me to say summat. But I've made one mistake letting me tongue have a free role already this season, so I'm keeping schtum. Rodney has advised me to say not one word to anyone until he's sealed a 'DARREN TACKLE VICTIM OF ESTABLISHMENT CONSPIRACY' exclusive with one of the posh papers. Sadly there's no sign yet of that Gabby Yorath off-of Sky Sports fetching up outside my gaff. Vow of silence or not, I'd give her an exclusive for nowt any day.

After the usual scrum trying to get out the house (only two reporters ended up in the ornamental pond, which is well down on me record) I'm cheered up no end when I get to training by this stroke Wattsy pulls on the returning Carmine.

It's his first day with the lads since coming back from his exile in South America, right, and Carmine's walked in at the start telling us about how he wants away to a big club on the continent, how he won't be ready for the World Cup if he carries on hanging out with a bunch of losers like us. How we're all pig ignorant. You know, the usual stuff. Kind of thing that makes us welcome him with open switchblades.

Well, after training, Carmine's mobile goes off (plays the tune of the Paraguayan national anthem, so he tells us). He answers it and his face is a picture. He's started giving it 'yes Signor Souness, no Signor Souness, that money sound very, very nice for me, Signor Souness'. Then he comes off the blower and starts tangoing round the dressing room singing 'Y Viva España'.

'Hey, you lot of losers,' he goes. 'It's bye-bye and goodnight from Carmine. I'm, how you say, slinging my hook from the Daihatsu for ever and stepping out into the Stadium of Light. Yes, Graeme Souness he call me, wants to re-build Benfica around my, what he call, cultured left foot. Carmine, he say: adios, arsewipes, thank you very much indeed. Now he runs with the big knobs.'

With that he's gone and out. Two minutes later, Wattsy swans into the dressing room, grin wider than Paul Scholes's arse. Graeme Souness was only him, wasn't it, on his mobile in the shower room giving it the old Sean Connery accent routine.

'I leave him to stew, Moneypenny,' he goes. 'Break the news to him in what, five, six weeks?'

Wednesday 5th

I'm on the blower to Rodders, first thing after training (new stretching and spinning exercises Old Demo picked up from watching the American women's lacrosse team train). What I needs is more input, finance-wise. There is a real requirement round my way for a couple of new signings. Preferably at the bottom of big cheques.

When I gets through to Rods, instead of him, some right wuss answers.

'Rodney's not at home right now,' this wuss goes. 'Whom may I say is calling him?'

I tell him.

'Oooh, Dazza. What an utter thrill. I'm Tristram, Rodney's new aide-de-camp.'

His what?

'Assistant. I give him assistance. Anyhow, I'm thrilled to say we have met before.'

I assure him we haven't: I'd've remembered meeting someone called Tristram.

'No, no, no. Cast your mind back and you'll remember.'

'Listen, mate, as a top Premier league star, I meet so many folk,' I says. 'But I've never met you. Now where's Rodders? It's rather urgent.'

'Dazz, I'm hurt,' this Tristram goes. 'Does the name Fi-Fi the Flounder not ring a few bells?'

You what?

'I see it does,' he goes. 'Then, let me reveal to you that I am none other than the Greens' cuddly match mascot herself. Well, me and several hundredweight of latex. And it takes all my training to exude in that costume, I can tell you. That's how I met Rodney, when I was being Fi-Fi. It was two weeks ago today, at a charity auction of signed balls. Though sadly yours were not among them. Our eyes met across a crowded urinal and he said come work with me. Don't tell me you don't now remember your little trysts with Trist? Or should I say: Fi-Fi?'

Oh bloody hell fire.

Thursday 6th

The Carmine joke continues.

After training, Bob dumps one of his steaming specials into a plastic bag, and pops it into the glove compartment of Carmine's Ferrari while the geezer himself is busy telling the Boss that he must be put in charge of team selection.

'Obviously, as I say, that is the only way Carmine stay here at the Daihatsu,' I overheard him saying to the Boss. 'I had that Graeme Souness on the, how you say, blower again today. He say he desperate very much indeed for Carmine.'

Not when Souey gets a whiff of his motor he won't be.

Friday 7th

After training (positional awareness exercise Demo spotted observing Uruguayan polo-players train) I'm flicking through the papers for news of my attempt to join the fake tartan trail and into the Scotland squad in time for the World Cup, when I spots some article about how much top sportsmen are earning these days. Sort of jumps out at me, with the frame of mind I'm in at the moment. Eye-opener it is and all, discovering what Damon Hill and Lennox Lewis take home. But the killer in the list is the number nine position.

'Here, lads, what do you think old Les Ferdinand's pulling down?' I says.

'What,' says Vic. 'Other than Dani Behr?'

'Says here £1.6 million a year. What's that a week?'

None of us has a calculator, but it's not peanuts, is it? I mean, not bad for lying around all day on the treatment table. According to the paper, most of it's down to endorsements, so I'm straight on the blower to Rodders. Seems to me the geezer's really not exploiting me enough. A footballer's career's short, and basically a boot deal's just not sufficient in this competitive new world. I'm looking for a computer game, a record and a tie-in with a fashion house (Gucci would be tidy). Plus books. Sure I've had one out earlier on in my career, and then there's this one, but Shearer has about ten a year, and they're all about as exciting as a night on the town with John Motson.

Course he's not there, Rods. And I gets that bloody Tristram again.

'Where's Rodney?' I says.

'A trifle brusque this morning, Mr T, if I might say so.'

'No you bloody can't. Now where is he?'

'Seeing as it's you, I'll tell you. He's out trying to sign up a new client.'

Not to put too fine a point on it, I am gob-smacked. How come the geezer's got time to lavish on someone else when frankly the off-the-park activities of yours truly are looking distinctly knob?

'Who?'

'Haven't you heard, Mr T? It's that Les Ferdinand.'

Monday 10th

Rodders finally rings back. I tell him what the situation is: either the dosh starts to flow, Les-style, or I'm off to join Eric Hall. I mean, everywhere you look these days there's players getting their noses in the trough. Besides, after yet another weekend without a bleedin' win bonus, things is beginning to look a bit stretched.

'I'm distressed you is unhappy, boy,' says Rodders. 'What can Rodders do for you? We're in this together, boy.'

I says, what about *Hello!* magazine? Les Ferdinand's just done that, and Teddy Sheringham. They even had

Jason Cundy from Ipswich in there. Word in the dressing-room is you pull down 30 long 'uns for showing them lot round your lovely home. Not exactly a strenuous afternoon's work, is it? I mean, I tell Rods, it's well up my alley. Especially as 30 long 'uns would come in nice and handy right now.

'Bit difficult with your place, boy,' says Rodders. 'I mean, speaking solely as your best friend, your gaff is pants. The whole geseft looks like the Indian government's been round testing a nuclear device in your khazi.'

I could get me mam in, I says. Get her to clear out a few of the Pot Noodle cartons and that.

'No, boy,' he goes. '*Hello!* are looking for something that says "lifestyle" and "aspiration". Not something that says "mock Tudor" or "executive cul-de-sac". Think on.'

Tuesday 11th

I've slept on it and have decided to get myself a new place to live. I bought this place with LeeAnne, the ex-bird, and it's full of memories of her: the broken mirror where she chucked her stiletto at me; the knife-mark in the kitchen where she lunged at me after the Supporters' Club Award Night when one of my legion of fans got a bit fresh. You know, memories. Besides, Rodders is right, as a professional, image is everything. And I should look on the property as an investment long-term. After all, there's *OK* as well as *Hello!* magazine.

Besides, if I move, I can get rid of one or two hangers-on. And I'm not thinking of the press scum outside the front door. Last photographer left this morning, off to David Ginola's place, apparently, everyone looking for a hair-washing shot. No. I'm talking me stepfather. He's been a bleedin' fixture round my way since I mentioned to me mam about the damp problems in the conservatory.

'You want to get Donald round, pet,' she says. 'He's a dab hand with the old Polyfilla.'

So I gives him a set of keys to let himself in a couple of month back and the geezer's never been out the place. Every afternoon when I come back from training, hoping to put in a bit of quality rest in front of a video of *101 Golden Green Moments* (including my thirty-yard thriller against Liverpool in my debut season), he's bleedin' there. Usually with a few mates from down his club, playing snooker.

'This is Wayne, lad,' he gives it when I walk in, pointing out some flabby guts in head-to-toe thread nightmare. Or: 'Geoffrey, may I introduce to you my esteemed stepson, Mr Darren Tackle.'

I mean, I accept that meeting the punters is part and parcel of the game these days and usually I'm prepared to show a bit of good grace, even at the training ground when, to be honest, Tacklemania can get a bit out of hand sometimes. As we professionals never forget, the punters is the ones paying our wages.

In the privacy of me own home, though, being presented with a procession of layabout middle-aged yonners brought round by me stepfather, all wanting a slice, is going a bit far. Specially as when we was growing up, this Donald wanted sod all to do with me, Lee and Clayton except when he had the occasional need of a punch-bag. Course, the moment I sign professional forms, he's all over me like a River Street slapper, wanting tickets, wanting invites to do's. Now all he wants is for me to bring me team-mates home after training.

'Any chance of fetching that Carmine back tomorrow, lad?' he says only last week. 'I'm sure he'd benefit from five minutes of wisdom, Donald-style.'

Not if the geezer wanted to learn about Polyfilla he

wouldn't. Turns out Donald can't even do that properly. Where Mr Chairman's company left a gaping hole in me conservatory, now there's enough cement to repoint Hadrian's Wall. Turns out me stepdad is the Graham Taylor of DIY.

Anyhow, as well as staying one step ahead of Donald, a new house could make a new statement about me. Show that I am projecting a new image, you know like Robbie Fowler and the Liverpool lads, what *FHM*, when they done that interview with me last month, called 'post-Scally'.

So what I needs on the house front is something classy. I want something top-notch and tasteful: electronic gates, video surveillance, stabling, brick-built path with checkerboard patterning, one of them baronial double staircases like Kenny Dalglish has in them BT ads. Plus a big atrium up front so you can stand on the balcony of your bedroom in your robe and look down on the snooker table. As I say: stylish.

So, after training, I goes to an estate agent in town and tells them the figure I was looking to spend. To be honest, she's quite a tidy bit of crump, the estate agent bird, giving it 'Mr Tackle this', and 'Sir that'. And she recommends we look out in the posh villages down past the airport: you know, all Range Rovers and bored housewives having affairs with their tennis coaches. I think: I'll have some of that. First off is this massive place what, from the picture, looks like a castle.

Wednesday 12th

The best time for me to view the house is after training, so I spin over in me training gear in the Jeep (which, to be honest, could do with a clean, but me mam's got a bit of the old lumbago at the moment). When the owner opens the door, she takes one look at me, clocks the Jeep and tells me I can start in the paddock. No idea what she's on about, but I wander out into this field behind the garage anyway where there's a couple of bleedin' horses getting a trifle frisky for my liking. While I'm trying to avoid a costly injury from a flailing hoof, the estate agent arrives and tells me the owner only thinks I'm the landscape gardener.

Anyhow, the misunderstanding is cleared up, but you could tell the owner was well unhappy about showing me round. It was all 'do you mind not touching that' and 'would you mind taking your shoes off in this room, I really don't want horsey business on my Wilton'. She says this as we walks into this massive room – same size as the gym at the training ground, except with this big-like wood table in it, with candlesticks and that on the walls.

'Lovely room for entertaining,' says the estate agent bird. 'And through these lovely patio doors, the views go all the way down to the building works for the new runway. Exceptional room for dinner parties, don't you agree, Mr Tackle?'

'S'pose so,' I says. 'Still, be handy for the snooker table.'

Top-notch gaff, all round, as it happens. Specially if you took out all them bookshelves. Afterwards, while we're walking back to our cars, the estate agent turns to me and says, 'Mr Tackle, I hope you don't mind me talking to you like this.'

Well, frankly love, I says, a dolly like you can talk to me anyway you like. Makes a change, after LeeAnne, to meet a bird what's not a puncher. Or a slapper.

'It's just that, well, I don't think in this market you will be taken seriously if you turn up looking so – how can I put this – *déshabillé*.'

You what?

'Might I suggest you invest in some smarter clothes and perhaps borrow a more appropriate car?'

So I put me mind to it on the drive home and decide, sod it, let's do this thing properly. What does Giggsy drive? Answer: one of them new Aston Martin DB7s. Where does Giggsy live? Answer: some massive gaff with stabling out in the countryside. Are the two connected? Answer: yes.

So I'm straight on the mobile, flog the Beamer and order a DB7 in Acapulco Gold with tangerine Connolly leather seats. Ninety-five long 'uns, the salesman geezer tells me, make it cash upfront and he'll throw an extra spoiler on the back for bobbins. Be with me within ten weeks.

Then, I have a quick trip to that new Gianni Versace showroom in Cross Street and walk out three suits heavier, and about fifteen G's lighter. These are clothes that say: money.

Now let's see some snobby cow in the stockbroker belt sneer at Darren Tackle.

Thursday 13th

The Carmine joke has reached its conclusion.

We're all in the physio room, discussing groin strains with Suzette, except Carmine who's out on the training pitch undermining the entire morale of the dressing-room by putting in some extra work on his own, when Wattsy gets out his mobile.

'Gentlemen,' says Wattsy. 'I think the time is right for some laughter therapy.'

He dials Carmine, who answers straight off (least the geezer's clocked footballers' rule number one: never leave the mobile in the changing-room, you never know what endorsement you might miss). And Wattsy then gives it his full Kevin Keegan number.

'Carmine, I want you at Fulham.'

Carmine says something we can't hear.

'Of course, you may not think that Fulham is an adequate platform for your skills, but let me tell you that Mr Al Fayed, the owner, is desperate to build his club around you.'

Carmine says something else we can't hear.

'Mr Al Fayed is the owner of Harrods.'

Carmine speaks.

'It's a shop.'

Carmine again.

'Yes, it is only a shop, but it's a very expensive one and Mr Al Fayed is very keen that you should play for Fulham. I tell you how keen he is, Carmine, he is prepared to give you not only twice what you are making at the Daihatsu, but to throw in a set of Harrods vouchers, a Christmas hamper for your mother plus priority booking in the queue for Santa's grotto. How does that sound?'

Wattsy's just about to get round to the bit about a supermarket sweep round the fourth floor Ralph Lauren concession when the door to the physio room bursts open and in comes Carmine, brandishing his mobile phone, which he proceeds to attempt to insert between Wattsy's buttocks. And if it wasn't for Vic, Bob, me and Darko, he might well have succeeded. This is not a happy bunny.

'You think I know fuck nothing about what you doing!' screams Carmine in the ensuing handbags. 'But I tell you I know fuck everything you try to do to me. How you say, I know fuck all!'

He then storms out, straight to the car-park and jumps

in his Ferrari. As Bob points out, possibly not the most fragrant place to get away from it all at the moment.

Friday 14th

Yes! I got the big call-up today. Forget Hoddle, forget McCarthy, forget the bleedin' Scottish FA (which is just as well, as that's what they seem to be doing to me): this is the spanker. I have been invited on *They Think It's All Over*.

'I'm proud of you, boy,' Rodders says when he rings with the news. 'I made you what you is today. I put you on the road. And now this. The pinnacle for any pro. I'm made up, boy. If only my mum was alive to share this moment with me. I tell you, boy. There's a lump in Rodders' throat.'

Me, I'm already beginning to wallow in the dressing-room cred that will follow as I spar humorously with Nick Hancock, make a couple of gags about the boss to Rory McGrath and put that Gary Lineker right in his place.

Monday 17th

The papers are full of Carmine's latest runner. He's back in Paraguay licking his wounds and whingeing to the assembled jackals that he wants away. Me, I think we're better off without him. Well, that's not strictly true as he's the only bastard at our place what can put the ball in the net at the moment. But scoring goals isn't everything in football. And morale-wise, with him gone, we're well in credit.

Not that I've got the time to worry about that now. I'm

down to London for more important matters. The telly beckons: Darren Tackle, Media Star.

When I get to the studio for the *They Think It's All Over* recording, I'm met at the reception by this dolly with a clipboard and an accent what could cut cheese at forty paces.

'Ah yes, Darren Tackle,' she says, all la-di-da, speaking really loud and slow. 'You're in dressing-room seven. Turn left at reception and follow the corridor round.'

I'm not deaf, I says.

'Possibly not,' she says. 'But I'm just making sure you understand. You are, after all, a footballer.'

Once in the dressing-room I'm faced with a right dilemma. I've brought meself a few top items from the wardrobe and I'm not altogether sure: should it be casual – Armani T-shirt, perhaps – or should it be smart? And if I go smart, should I go smart smart with a tie or smart casual without? After trying on a full seven permutations, eventually I decide to go casual smart, teaming a handy Yves Saint Laurent top in Prussian Cherry with the Nehru-collared suit in Madagascan Mauve what I picked up at Versace's earlier in the week. Says something about me, I reckon, as I check out the final look in the mirror.

I've only just had time for a swift gargle of the old mouthwash when the posh bint turns up, telling me it's time to go on set.

'My, my,' she says, eyeing me up as I open the door. 'That is a busy ensemble.'

Reckon I'm in there for laters.

I've been put on Baldy and Posho's team, while Hairy and Big Ears have got some student comedian what supports Chelsea. We're all lined up behind the set while the warm-up geezer is going through his paces getting the audience all excited when that Nick Hancock sidles up to me and says: 'Have you got a volume control for that outfit, Dazz?'

Now, when it comes to banter, you don't try it on with a footballer, well-versed as he is with the repartee and crack of the professional dressing-room. Hancock probably thinks he's had some in the comedy clubs, but that's as nothing compared to what goes on at our place, the laughs you have and that. So I comes straight back at him with the well-drilled, final put-down, the kind of response learnt after a thousand bouts of dressing-room wordplay: 'Shut it, gobshite.'

As the cameras start to roll, I have to admit to being a touch nervous. But give him his due, that Hancock, he soon makes me feel better by ripping the piss out of the wuss Chelsea comedian from the off. Top-drawer stuff.

Then he turns to me and makes a couple of jokes about me having to come on the show to help pay off the fines. I let it pass because it's a comedy show and you've got to have a sense of humour in this game. Though I don't know what he's talking about, with the bleedin' fee the BBC hands over, I'd have to appear every night for ten years to pay off what I owe.

Anyhow, things are going all right – I've set out my stall, saying nowt, letting the Chelsea bloke make a right carpet of himself – till they get to that 'Feel the Sportsman' round.

'Now normally at this point in the show,' says Hancock, 'Lee Hurst and David Gower don the blindfolds, but this week, to mark the visit of our special guest Darren Tackle, we're going to ask him to put one on instead and step out there.'

And he hands me a blindfold. Well, I know when the mystery guest walks in, because there's a huge cheer. I'm hoping it's Sharron Davies, so I goes straight to the tit area and come up instead with a load of nylon football shirt. So I'm grabbing it, but I've no idea who it is.

'Don't you know, Dazz?' Hancock's saying. 'I can't believe you don't.'

Well, I'm floundering, putting on this big grin pretending I'm having a lark, while me insides are flapping around like David James under a high cross. And that Hurst isn't any help, just making a bunch of lame jokes about thighs and that. The time's ticking away and I'm getting nowhere except to realise there's more than one person and they seem to be wearing some sort of football kit.

'Really no idea, Dazz?' Hancock says and the audience howls with laughter when I clearly gets meself a handful of footballer's cods. Then, before I know what's happening, time's up and I take the blindfold off and there, larger than bleedin' life, is Wattsy, Vic, Bob, Bubbles, Hermann and the rest of the lads.

When everyone's finished cheering and shaking hands and that, I'm just handing over me blindfold to Hancock when he says: 'I suppose we shouldn't be surprised Darren Tackle doesn't recognise his colleagues while wearing a blindfold. After all, he's spent his entire career failing to pick out his team-mates with a ball at his feet and his eyes wide open . . .'

Wednesday 19th

On the way into training I get a call on the mobile from Adele, saying the Boss wants me in his office. I think I know why. I walks in and his twitch is full on.

'Fucken fuck fucker,' he says, pushing the morning's papers over towards me. 'Fuckenell. Eh? Eh? Fuckenell.'

He's upset, I can tell.

And there's why, in full colour: 'NEW SOCCER SHOCKER: DAZZA IN LIVE TELEVISION BRAWL' says the headline in the *Sun*. 'Full amazing story pages 2, 3, 4, 5, 6, 17, 18, 56, 57, 58.'

In the *Mirror* it's: 'THEY THINK IT'S ALL OVER: IT IS NOW FOR DAZZA'.

But the *Mail*'s the worst: 'Soccer star Darren "Dazza" Tackle brought shame on the game last night when he aimed a punch at host Nick Hancock during the hit quiz show *They Think It's All Over*. Luckily, Nick, 35, ducked out of the way of the blow, but a spokesman for the BBC said some minor damage was done to the set behind where he was standing. Afterwards Darren, 25, was taken to hospital with a suspected fracture of the right hand.'

'I'm sorry, Boss,' I says. 'I'll just hold me hand up and say I'll pay the fine.'

'Fuckenell. Eh? Eh? Hold your fucken hand up? Eh? Fuckenell, it's in fucken plaster,' he splutters. 'This is all I fucken need what with us out the Coca-Cola, rock bottom in the Premiership and our best player driven out by a bunch of fucken shit-lovers. Obviously I'm going to fucken fine you.'

Knob.

'But it's not for fucken trying to fucken hit Hancock.'

You what?

'It's for not fucken hitting him properly. The whole of football's been looking to twat that smug git for months and when you get the chance, who is it who ends in casualty? You, you fucken incompetent. Now fucken get out of here. Fuckenell.'

Let's hope he doesn't find out about the damage I did to the club motor trying to run over Lee Hurst in the car-park afterwards.

Thursday 20th

Still, there's always the new house to cheer me up. I've decided I'm deffo on the move. Got home yesterday after the rollocking from the Boss and only found Donald had gone and taped over *Pick of the Greens: 1958–1998. The best all-time action from Wally 'Kid' Waldron to Darren 'Dazza' Tackle*. The lot disappeared. And for what? The Regal Welsh Snooker Open from Prestatyn, that's what.

All in all then, I was well chuffed to get a call on the mobile on the way into training this morning from the estate agent bird. She's got some swanky new place to sell, fresh instruction, she says, that came in this very morning. It's got everything, she says, from an in-built sauna in the cellar to a clock tower over the treble garages. She says I can meet her round there as soon as I've changed after training. So I asks her how much the gaff is. And she tells me.

'Ah,' I says. 'I think that's a little out of my price range.'

'But that's the price you told me you were able to go to,' she says, sounding, I might add, a little disappointed.

'I know,' I says. 'But that was before.'

'Before what?'

'Before I spent most of me money on the new motor and the suits.'

DECEMBER

Monday 1st

It's important, obviously, as professionals, that when things start to go wrong, we the players sit down as a group of lads together and share some of the responsibility. This means being prepared to accept frankly and openly that the situation at the Daihatsu is just not acceptable at the moment. We're looking well ragged at the back, decidedly thin up front; not sure, as a unit, whether to go long or short.

It's not yet Christmas, but the situation is getting that serious: we are a club in hair crisis. In truth, we're all over the place barnet-wise. Some have got the old Beckham wet-look, Vic's gone for a dinky Ian Walker bob, a couple of the older lads are moving towards the Attilio Lombardo-style major centre parting. No doubt about it, we need a new direction.

It was Wattsy what said some of us clued-up lads had to set an example, take the lead. He told us about this barber called the Hobo. This is a new-wave hairdresser, apparently, calls himself a scalp mechanic and works in a warehouse full of industrial machinery just behind the station. So, after training, I get Rodney straight on the mobile to sort me a booking. Except, as is his growing habit, he's not there. So that Tristram, or whatever he calls himself, does it for me.

'Anything to oblige, Mr T,' he says. And I get the nasty feeling he means it.

Tuesday 2nd

When I walk in to this Hobo's, I'm nearly deafened by Dutch hard-core house and some surly welfare-to-work bird yelling at me asking me if I've got an appointment. I says I have and she only goes and asks what the name is. What's wrong with these people, asking me my name? Doesn't everyone read *Loaded*?

I'm plonked in this big dentist-style chair in front of a mirror, have a towel whipped round me collar, and me neck bent double over a massive old sink what looks as though no one's been near it with any Jif for a month. Kind of domestics me mam would throw a wobbler at if she saw. Then another surly bird in top-knot, parachutist kex and fat-arsed shoes sprays me locks like I'm on the full gold-medal valet service down at the Tesco's car wash. When that's done, she starts pummelling at me head. And I mean pummelling. Where, I can't help thinking, are the fingers of the lovely Suzette when I needs them most?

'I thought this was meant to be relaxing,' I shouts over the decibels.

'Eh?' she yells back.

'I says I thought this was meant to be relaxing.'

'Yer what?'

I'm just about to give it the old 'Do you know who I am?' routine – something we pros reserve only for the most dire emergencies – when me train of thought is disturbed by the arrival of this tramp in me line of mirror vision. Not only has the security in this gaff gone completely awry to let the fella in, but he walks straight over and starts fingering at me hair. I mean this place is supposed to be exclusive. What's going on?

'I'm Hobo,' this tramp yells, and I should've walked there and then. He looks like one of them hedge monkeys currently tunnelling under the intended path of the new runway, all dreadlocks and Catweazle beard and half the crown jewels embedded in his facial orifices. And when he starts droning on about radically altering the aesthetic perceptions of the modern athlete, I should have definitely upped and gone. But I didn't. Trouble was, by the time he got out the garden shears it was too late.

Wednesday 3rd

Of course, to the so-called new-wave hairdresser, it was just a slip of the wrist in the final rinse. He can have no idea that to the highly honed athlete, a bottle of bleach in the wrong hands is a total disaster. They say that football is a game played nine-tenths in the mind. And I'd have to agree with that. Can you imagine what serious style-related jip the muppets in the opposition end are going to give me the moment I trots out in banana-coloured hair? Can you really comprehend the damage – psychologically speaking – to the modern professional sportsman? How else do you explain David James's torment if it isn't that the geezer lost it after an interface with three thousand baying Man U. fans and a sachet of L'Oréal 'Simply Natural' in an unhappy shade of magenta?

Course, the moment I turn up at training this morning, they're all in there, pissing theirselves at me bonce like we're all back at bleedin' school. I mean, what's Old Grandad got to snigger about, that's what I'd like to know. Even Michael Bolton doesn't wear a Michael Bolton cut these days.

Wattsy's straight in there too, giving it plenty.

'Oooh, which poodle parlour did the Dog go to for that particular clipping?' was one of his choicer efforts.

Now I come to think of it, he should bloody know where I went. It was him what recommended this Hobo in the first place.

Anyhow, after two hours of bollocks as Darren Tackle becomes the Nicky Butt of every gag, I'm straight off to the Boss's office to tell him I'm really not mentally fit for this Saturday. Not against Leeds. Imagine what 2,000 travelling Yorkie satirists in their end will make of my barnet. I walk in past Adele, who seems to have some sort of cold problem, because the moment she sees me she starts making a snuffling noise behind her hands, and you know what the first thing the Boss says is?

'Fuckenell, Dazz.'

Then it's: 'What you got on your fucken head? A dead fucken polar bear or what? Eh?'

I tell him I'm out for this coming Saturday. Just wouldn't be able to do meself justice with this head on.

'Fuckenell, eh? It's fucken Wednesday,' he says. 'The game's on fucken Saturday. Gives you three days to get it fucken dyed fucken back, Dazz. Now fucken, you know, piss off.'

Which only goes to show there's not so much a generation gap as a massive yawning chasm between the boss class and the players in football these days: any face worth their Gucci strides will tell you two dyes in a week is a complete no-no as far as root maintenance is concerned.

Thursday 4th

Donald is now a permanent fixture indoors. I gets home from training, hoping to catch up with a few zeds in front of *Jerry Springer*, only to find him and half a dozen of his drinking mates parked in front of pro-celebrity pool on Sky Sports 3, noshing out on my week's supply of Jaffa Cakes.

'Blimey, lad,' he says as I walk in. 'You all right? Who

done this to you, son? Want me and the boys to go round and sort him out?'

'Donald,' I says. 'It's a haircut. It's not an opportunity for you to go out and act like it's Brighton sea front, 1963 all over again.'

'An 'aircut?'

'Yes.'

'What, deliberate and that?'

'No, Donald, I was mugged at hair-drier point by a marauding gang of trainee hairdressers, who held me down and committed a serious assault on me follicles.'

'You didn't pay for it?'

'I did.'

'How much?'

'£207.'

'Stone me, lad. We'll definitely go out and do him. A lad in your position shouldn't let anyone take liberties.'

Yeah, and when it comes to taking liberties Donald should know. He's got seven GCSEs in piss-taking.

Saturday 6th

Being a professional, of course, I am prepared to go the extra mile in the team's cause. And when the Boss points out that what with my hair, Vic spraining an ankle falling off his new Red or Dead wedge-heels and Bob suffering from lock-jaw after cosmetic dentistry, we are plunged deep into an injury crisis at precisely the wrong time, I tell him I'm willing to take on board the jip and play. Specially when the alternative is three weeks' wages in fines.

As it happens, I wish I hadn't bowed to me better instincts. I should've stuck to me guns and told the Boss I wasn't fit for it. But once I'm in the dressing-room and he's started on his pre-match pep talk, I haven't got a hope of getting out.

'Eh? Eh?' he starts. And then he's off on one of his legendary psyche-ups. The media and that, they always ask you, what did the Boss say before this match or that match to make you come out like that. Since everyone's so interested, I can exclusively reveal in full what he said today. And it was:

'Fuckenell. Eh. Eh? Get fucken stuck fucken in from the fucken off. Eh? Fucken don't give fucken nothing away. And if any fucken, you know, fucker, gets fucken past yer, fucken do him. Eh? Eh? Cooomon. Cooomon. Fuckenell.'

I tell you, you'd walk through walls for the fella after a gee-up like his. We was all up for it, slapping each other on the back, shaking hands. Ready to get out there and sweat 110 per cent for the Greens. And as we trot out, I reckon it's going to go all right, I'll be able to deflect any hair-directed criticism from the stands. Though the ref wasn't happy, I convinced him I had some tender scar tissue on the top of me head, and that the baseball cap was for added protection. With one or two minor slippage scares, throughout the first half, the cap does its job and just about covers the Hobo's handiwork.

Second half, different story. With no Carmine – geezer's still sulking in South America – it was hell out there, constant bloody pressure. The Boss's words are soon drowned out by the onslaught. Up front, one of the Bosnians simply can't hold it; Wattsy and Bubbles are getting over-run in midfield, and Gary 'Bollocks' Ball has a right bollocks of a game in front of me. I tell you how shite he is today, everytime I pass it up the line to him, he keeps letting the ball go way over his head.

It's relentless, and in the end, the only breather I gets is when I'm substituted in the 63rd minute. It happened after an almighty scramble in our box. During this, I get an elbow in the face (which the ref, as per the usual anti-Green instructions the FA hand out before games, pretends not to see) and the cap flies off. Just at the point I'm bending down to pick it up, Darko is endeavouring a suicidal back pass to Hermann and the only goal of the game creeps through me open legs. The Boss is right on his feet: 'Fuckenell. Eh? Eh?'

Next thing I knows, me number's being held up by Demo on the electronic board and I'm off, replaced by the other Bosnian, the one who's put on three stone since he come to England. Unfortunately all this happens right under the gaze of the Hyundai North Stand, where the away fans are gathered. And I'm forced to walk off, head down, cap back on, to the assembled multitude of Leeds yonners chanting 'Are you Jimmy Savile in disguise?' Then, I'm forced to spend the rest of the match on the bench listening to the occupants of the Platinum Club seats behind the dug-out giving it plenty.

'Hoy, Tackle,' one of them shouts and I turns round to see this geezer, in collar and tie and all, legless, just about swaying to his feet. 'You're fucking useless, you peroxide prat. Day you were conceived, your father would have done us all a favour if he'd just had a wank.'

And they say modern-day football's pricing out the yobs.

Afterwards, you could have started a boy scout's camp-fire off of the atmosphere in the dressing-room. Without a win in the Premiership, we are getting well used to the sight of everyone else's arses disappearing over the horizon. The Boss is not in the jolliest of moods.

'Fuckenell' is all he can say for the first three minutes, before deciding the best course of action is to make a single-handed assault on the world crockery-abuse record. In this sort of mood we know just to sit there and take it. So even when he's started chucking the contents of the kit skip around, we all sit there in silence. When a jockstrap lands on my head, I don't flinch an inch. Until he sees me.

'Fuckenell, eh? Tackle? Eh? What the fuckenell are you doing, you fucken cream-headed ponce?' he says. 'Let the ball through your fucken legs and then have the nerve to sit there through a bollocking with an athletic support on your head. Fuckenell. Right, you're doing the fucken random fucken drugs test.'

Knob, knob and thrice knob. This is the last thing I need, what with the night I had on Thursday, when I went into town to get away from Donald and his pals and ended up bumping into Marco, who, fortunately, had the wherewithal to help me get me head back together. Anyhow, when the Boss has disappeared in a twister of steam, I ask Wattsy what I'm supposed to do. I've got more Gianluca floating around in my system than a member of the all-Colombia formation line-dance team. Luckily he's come up with a couple of handy tips.

'I know it sounds unlikely after the performance the Dog has just given,' he says, 'but tell the duty doctor you've sweated too much to cock your leg on his lamp-post just now. Then get down to the players' lounge, sink three or four pints, and your urine sample'll be so full of booze they won't be able to trace owt in there.'

Top man in a crisis, Wattsy.

Ten minutes later I'm just on me way from the lounge gents up to the medical room, having filled one of them wine carafes from behind the bar to bursting, when I bumps into Old Demo in the corridor.

'I've been looking for you,' he says. 'It's your turn to entertain the clients in the Platinum Club lounge.'

'Bloody hell,' I says, holding up the sample. 'I'm off to the medical room.'

'Well, if I was you I'd get up there pronto,' he says. 'Mr Chairman's up there and all.'

Every cloud. Now this is the perfect opportunity to

make amends for the goal-line cock up, show I can still do a tip-top job for the club in the ever-more vital corporate entertaining area of the game. So I stroll into the Allied Dunbar lounge, pop me sample in the fridge behind the bar for safe keeping and wander over to where some of the better-heeled clientele are chatting to Mr Chairman. And stone me, when I get there one of them's only the drunken wassock who was giving me jip earlier.

'Ah, return of the custard head,' the wuss says, putting his arm round me. 'Your timing off the park is slightly better than on it. Me and Mr Chairman was only just talking about you, your bonce and that bloody soft goal.'

'I have to hold me hand up,' I says, trying to look all magnanimous and that for Mr Chairman. 'I should've kept me legs together.'

'Not you son,' comes back the geezer. 'Your mother.'

Now I'm not one to hold a grudge, but while they're all pissing theirselves – including, I might add, Mr Chairman – I slip to the fridge and pop back with my carafe of something cheeky.

'Fancy some of the club's new own-label white wine?' I ask the geezer. 'Slightly on the room-temperature side, I admit. But that's how they're serving it in Quaglino's these days.'

'Mr Tackle, do not believe a word they are saying about you,' geezer says, pouring himself and Mr Chairman a stiff one. 'You, sir, are an officer and a gentleman.'

Always happy to have been of service.

Sunday 7th

Off to me mam's for a touch of TLC. After the wassock in the *People* gives me a three for yesterday's effort, I needs someone to lick me wounds and at the moment it appears Gabby Yorath's just not available. I park the Jeep outside mam's gaff, but just before I pop in, I decide to stroll round for a couple of relaxing drinks down me old local – the Ferret & Pie Stall – with a few of the lads I was at school with.

Now some people may be surprised that an athlete is prepared to have a bevvy. But when you're young and fit and training every day, you can soon run off the effects of a pint or two. Besides, as I say, the game's nine-tenths in the mind, and what I needs right now is some serious relaxation, get me head well away from the pressure. And the Ferry's the best place for it, help you forget the day-to-day stresses and strains of stardom.

See, the lads there are mates I've known all me life. Down there, they like me for who I am, not what I am. If you see what I mean. I reckon everyone what's made a success of their lives needs someone to help keep their feet on the ground. And there's a bunch of them you can always find in the Ferry when you needs them, ordinary lads with ordinary jobs: one drives a fork-lift at Texas Homebase; another sells household goods, oven gloves, car chammies, that kind of thing door to door; another can do you a nice tarmac job on your front drive. Like I say, ordinary blokes.

'Stone me, look what the cat's brought in,' says the fork-lift truck driver when I walks in. 'Mr High and Bloody Mighty has decided to grace our unworthy lives with his presence. Mind you, I'm surprised he dares show his face round here after yesterday's fiasco. And what the bloody hell's that bandana he's wearing? Who's he think he is? David Ginola?'

Like I said, these lads accept me like I'm an ordinary fella, too. They even let me sit with them, after I've handed out a few complimentaries for the Liverpool game, a couple of twists left over from the other night with Marco, plus a few autographed photos of Carmine I keep handy for such occasions.

'Yeah, and you can get the bloody bevvies in and all, flash tosser,' says the household goods salesman.

Anyhow, I'm just at the bar getting in the fourth round I've bought this session when I spots a bit of barney blowing up in the corner. And who's in the middle of it but me brother Clayton.

'Eh, that's Clayt,' I says to one of the lads what's just turned up, a trainee popcorn-maker down the leisure centre.

'Oh aye,' he says, not even bothering to look over at the off. 'Mine's a treble rum and black.'

Clayt in trouble, eh. No change there. Thing is, when we was growing up it was always one for all and all for one with me and our Lee and our Clayton. Except on the occasions when them two would batter me or when I'd gang up with one of them to batter the other. So, of course, moment I sees him in bother, instinct kicks in. Role model for hundreds of kids Darren Tackle may be, but when he sees kith and kin in aggro, he's straight in there. Trouble is, by the time I've bought the drinks, taken them over to the lads in the corner and gone back for a round of Scampi Fries, it's all over. Clayton's been chased off out the door by a couple of geezers who are spitting fire.

'Coomon then you snide slag!' one of them's shouting out the door as Clayton legs it out the car-park.

'Hey, hold up, hold up,' I says to this geezer. 'What's going on?'

'Fuck off,' he says, throwing me arm off his shoulder.

Then he looks at me more careful like.

'Oh, bloody hell, it's Darren Tackle,' he says. 'La-di-bloody-da. Sorry, sunshine, didn't recognise you with that poncey bandana round your head. What you wearing that for?'

'Got a bit of an 'ead injury, see,' I says. 'Anyhow, what's the trouble here?'

'I tell you what's the hassle, pal. We've had it with geezers coming in here trying to sell snide car parts. Course, you'll be reckoning yourself above that sort of thing now, but we've all had our cars done recently and we don't need it. So we told that wassock to sling it.'

'Yeah, well that wassock was my brother.'

'Bloody hell, that waster's your bro?' he goes. 'Now you come to mention it, I see the family resemblance: he was bloody slow when he ran off and all. By the way, any chance of tickets for the Liverpool game?'

The thing that marks a professional out from his peers is his ability to know his own body and its limits. So after eight pints, I'm off back to mam's, looking forward to one of her Sunday special dinners to soak it all up: deep-fried corned beef and chips, followed by mashed Creme Eggs and custard.

Then, as I'm getting near mam's house, something strange happens. At first I thought I was just, you know, ill with the ale, but I swear that the Jeep's looking about three foot higher off the ground than when I left it. There it is, sticking up well over the top of the hedge. And sure enough, when I've rounded the corner and I'm level with it, I see it's standing on four piles of bricks. While I was lubricating me tonsils, some little toe-rag's only made off with me special limited-edition BBS alloys.

'Mam,' I says, as I walks in. 'I've got to get you out of this neighbourhood.'

'Hold up, Darren pet,' she says. 'First things first. Why are you wearing a silk scarf round your head?'

'Mam, never mind that,' I says. 'This is ridiculous. I'm earning enough money to set you up somewhere decent. This area's full of scum. You're not safe here. Come and live at my gaff till we find you somewhere proper and that.'

'I don't want to go to your place, Darren pet,' she says. 'Not with your stepfather spending so much time there. Anyway, what's brought all this on?'

'Me engine, mam,' I says. 'Look at it. Someone's only gone and nicked all the wheels off it in broad daylight while I was down the Ferry.'

'Oh, I wouldn't worry about that,' she says. 'Our Clayton's just popped round to use the phone and I heard him telling one of his mates he'd got a spare set of Jeep wheels he was looking to sell. I'm sure he'd let you have them for a decent price.'

Monday 8th

Eleven hundred quid it cost me. Plus me last pair for the Liverpool game. The geezer from Exorzt-U-Like took three hours to get round to me mam's, then complained like bastard because he said I'd not paid for the exhaust they'd put on in the summer, so that was another £250.

Anyhow, while I'm waiting for him to arrive, I have to sit there watching the Sky game with Donald and three of his mates who was all making rare appearances outside the four walls of my gaff. As if it's not bad enough watching Man U. win again, he's there beside me on the sofa giving it plenty throughout the game about how modern-day footballers are soft as shite and how they couldn't pass their way out of a custard pie. Which was the last thing I wanted to hear, specially after what me mam had served up for Sunday dinner.

'Mam,' I'd said as she pops a banana on me plate, 'what's this?'

'It's a banana, pet.'

'Yes, I know that,' I says. 'But what about corned beef and chips? What about mam's special Creme Egg and custard?'

'No, pet,' she says. 'I seen that shouty chef on telly the other day and he says you footballers these days only eat bananas. Perfect for muscle fatigue or something.'

There's no arguing with her. So I'm that starving I have to stop off for a KFC on the way home.

All in all, this morning I'm not really in the mood for training. And to make matters worse, Demo's got some new exercises he borrowed from watching the Slovakian synchronised swimming team train, all deep breathing and standing on your bloody tip-toes while counting backwards in units of five. It's not exactly guaranteed to lift the gloom which has descended since Saturday's fiasco.

Which reminds me. Another bloody week without a win bonus. So immediately after training, I rings Rodney to check out how things are going on the extra-curricular earnings front. And, as per bloody usual, I gets that bloody Tristram, or whatever he's called.

'Mr T, long time no parley. What a thrill. How was my good friend the Hobo?'

'Rodders there?'

'A little bird tells me that your new look was an absolute visual triumph.'

'I said, is Rodders there?'

'A tetchy Mr T this morning, is it not? Since you ask, Mr Gee is out. But may I take a message?'

'Yeah, you can,' I says. 'Tell him his client would like to know how come he's never in when he needs him.'

'Well, I can tell you precisely where he is. He's out there getting the work in.'

'Not for bloody me he's not.'

'Well, Mr T, speaking solely in your best interests here, I must say, after the Barney Butcher débâcle and the Nick Hancock situation, the Darren Tackle line has not exactly been running hot here.'

'Yeah, well, you tell him what's a bloody agent for but to make it run hot.'

After all, I could do with an injection of long 'uns to help pay the hairdressing bills. I've just got back from Barnette's, that fancy salon in town. They told me the only way to get rid of the banana look was a number-one crop. They charged me £195 for the kind of slap-head that me mam used to give the three of us with grandad's clippers when we was kids for nowt.

Monday 15th

Carmine's back. The papers are full of how he's been reconciled with the club and how his girlfriend's decided she really likes it here and how the Boss has promised him that everything will be hunky and indeed dory from now on. Course, we all heard that the real reason he's showed up is the Paraguayan team manager has told him he's got no chance of making their World Cup squad unless he starts playing regular first-team football instead of hanging round the barrios complaining to any media man what wants to pass the time of day about England and the English. And, of course, there's not another club in Europe mug enough to take him on except the jolly Greens.

This morning, then, he turns up at training with his own personal trainer he's flown over from Acapulco, or some such, and tells us all he'll be working on his own from now on. Which upsets Old Demo no end. In an effort to please which might in a less tolerant environment be misconstrued as pathetic arse-licking, the old tosser's only just got back from a week-long fact-finding tour to South America to find out what we're doing wrong. So while Carmine's out there doing his own thing, we're all subjected to some new Latin stretching torture Demo reckons is the only way to stop the losing streak.

As it happens, though we may be rooted at the bottom of the Premiership, the atmosphere in the dressing-room's on the up. Nothing to do with Carmine's return, natch. It's just everyone buzzing off the World Cup draw. Hermann's jumping up and down about Norway landing the Jocks, Darko's full of how his Romanians will stuff England, and it turns out the fat Bosnian's been a Yugoslav all along and is an absolute deffo for a month in France. Even Bubbles and Wattsy are getting in on the act, telling us how they're off to join the Reggae Boyz of Jamaica, even though the closest either of them has ever been to the old country is that club down River Street, where Wattsy does a bit of DJing, spinning a few handy platters of a Wednesday night.

Me? Well, Darren Tackle's ready to give 110 per cent in anyone's cause. Though at the moment, it seems me options are shrinking. Not a dicky has been heard from Hoddle, the tartan trail seems a complete no-no and of course the Irish badly, some might say thoughtlessly, let the likes of me down by not even qualifying. I'm just hoping Rodney manages to let the relevant Kraut authorities know about me nan having a fling with a German PoW while she was serving in the women's land army in the war. Far-fetched, maybe. But – come to think of it – it might well explain some of me long-lost dad's more disciplinarian tendencies.

Tuesday 16th

I'm on me way home from training, looking forward to a much-needed afternoon on the sofa with the remote controls lined up in front of me, when I gets a call on the mobile from Bill, the fella from the *People*.

'Any comment?' he goes.

'Yeah,' I says. 'As a matter of fact I have got a comment. I'm never buying your paper again. Okay, so I let the only goal through me legs. But a three? What's going on?'

'No, no, Dazz,' he says. 'Not that. Any comment on the news.'

'What news?'

'Haven't you heard?'

'Heard what?'

'The Boss,' he says. 'He's got the chop.'

Wednesday 17th

We footballers are focused people. As pros, we take the comings and goings in the manager's dug-out with a pinch of salt. The media and that seem to think we're as obsessed as they are with the speculation about why this bloke's in and that bloke's out. Nothing could be further from the truth. As a pro, as long as you're picked for the team, you don't care who you're picked by. I'm sure I speak for the majority of my colleagues when I say what we all reckon about managers is this: they may come and they may go, but you can be sure of one thing. There'll always be another one along in the morning.

But bloody hell, the Boss. What's going on there, eh? I mean, blimey, he was like a father to us, we're all absolutely gutted. Except, for some reason, Carmine, who was dancing a cha-cha round the changing-room at training this morning.

'Hey, the Boss is gone,' he's shouting. 'He slung his hook. Carmine he say: piss off loser. I am sick of him being – how you say – in my ass all the time.'

It all happened yesterday. While we was out freezing our bollocks off on the training pitch listening to Old Demo droning on about how if you get your yin and yang into alignment, then you will develop total physical harmony, Mr Chairman called the Boss into his office and sacked him. Pronto. Just like that. Across the very desk where he gets his secretary to brush up on her oral dictation skills every Thursday night. Hard, or what? To tell a man he's fired to his face. What with Christmas coming and all. I mean what's wrong with the tried and tested footballing method of giving a Boss the heave-ho: you know, letting him read it on Teletext?

Course, the papers are full of it. Page after page of analysis of where it all went wrong. About how a team of multi-national talents found itself languishing at the bottom of the table. Geezer in the *Sun*'s going on and on about how the Boss blew it over the Carmine situation. About how you should never put all your eggs in the one basket, specially if it's a fragile Latin-temperamental-style basket.

Typically, the papers have got it all wrong as usual. It was Wattsy what filled us all in at a team meeting he called at Mad Mick O'Shea's pub after training.

'Forget what they're saying in the papers, gentlemen,' he says. 'The situation was more complex than has been reported. In short, it was sod-all to do with footballing matters.'

And then he was off, telling us all sorts of stuff what you'd never have known if you'd relied on the media and that for your information.

As we all knew, Mr Chairman and the Boss have loathed each other for months, ever since they fell out mysteriously during that fact-finding tour with members of the Newcastle board to Marbella last year. Well, after that, Mr Chairman had been looking for any chance to off-load the Boss and with us languishing at the foot of the table and dumped from the Coca-Cola, it seemed like the perfect oppo. Trouble was, the Boss knew too much about him.

'You mean the Thursday night shuffle over his in-tray?' I says.

'More than that, Dog,' says Wattsy.

And out it comes. There was the time Mr Chairman took a shine to the dance floor in the Allied Dunbar suite and had it dug up and put in round at that drinking club he owns down Cross Street. There was the time he took the groundsman off pitch duties in the middle of last season and had him relaying the lawn outside his mansion, while we was playing on a cabbage patch and blowing our UEFA Cup place with one almighty bobble which looped comically over Hermann in the last home game. And remember the fans' travel club? You know, the thing that he insisted got formed a couple of years ago after our lot rioted in the derby against the bastard Blue scum? Well, turns out it was a front all along. He made it use coaches from his own bus company at twice the going rate to transport the unwashed to away games. This is the kind of thing that would, if it got out, make the students what run the fanzine hot-tail it straight round to his gaff and smash all the windows. So the Boss had a hold on him.

'Anything else?' I says.

'As it happens, there is,' says Wattsy. 'Remember last year how all the personal appearance work suddenly dried up? None of us could work out why all that opening super-markets and doing the charity fashion-show circuit had dried up to a trickle? Well, it was because Mr Chairman was manning the phones in the commercial department, telling the punters the players weren't available and doing the gigs himself for a pony in cash.'

Knob. What with that and the Rodney situation, no wonder I'm getting sod-all in the bank.

'Anyhow, when the Boss had enough on him, he made him give him a five-year contract otherwise he was going to spill the beans.'

'So how do you know all this?' says Bubbles.

'The Boss gave us a ring last night and asked me to come round and help him pack,' says Wattsy. 'He'd been living in a house Mr Chairman owns, which he'd been told to vacate pronto. It all come out as we was popping his collection of Rothmans into a tea chest. He told us in absolute strictest confidence, mind. So I don't want none of you toe-rags ringing up the *People* and getting the 25 quid tip-off fee.'

'But what I don't understand,' I says, 'is how come Mr Chairman's suddenly decided to get rid of the Boss now. I mean, can't the geezer just blab it all?'

'Trouble is, me old Dog,' says Wattsy, 'the Boss has sort of lost the moral high ground. The Boss's other half would really have something to blub about if she heard some of the stuff Mr Chairman's found out recently.'

'Like what?' says Darko.

'Well, he discovered last week that the Boss was humping Old Demo's missus.'

'You are joking,' Vic says. 'I'd rather be at home to Auntie Palm than engage with Old Demo's trouble.'

'Admits he was up to his nuts in it,' says Wattsy. 'That's why Demo was always being sent round the world on fact-finding tours.'

'Bloody hell,' says Vic. 'You mean we was all suffering from Demo's sadistic new training techniques just so the Boss could get three points away?'

'It gets worse,' says Wattsy. 'Why do you think Carmine's back?'

'Obvious, World Cup, innit?' says Darko.

'No,' says Wattsy. 'He's returned because his girlfriend was desperate to get back to England.'

'But it was her what hated living here in the first place,' I says.

'Yeah. But that was before she started getting gaffered by the Boss.'

'You're having a bubble,' I says. 'She's top totty. And the Boss must be way over forty.'

'It's fact,' says Wattsy. 'Apparently they first got it together when he went over there trying to persuade Carmine to come back and gave her a shoulder to cry on.'

'So how did Mr Chairman find out?' says Vic.

'He owns the gaff Carmine's living in remember, been trying to sell it for ever. Well the other day he popped round there with a prospective buyer and found the Boss giving her one over the snooker table while wearing one of Carmine's Paraguayan international caps. It wasn't so much that they were shagging that pissed Mr Chairman off. It was the fact that the studded leather thong she was trussed up in had ripped the baize on his prize table. And to make matters worse, the prospective buyer only goes and asks the bird if she's got any signed photos of Carmine lying around handy. For his daughter, obviously.'

After that, apparently, the Boss was finished. It was just a matter of working out the going rate for mutual consent. Which settled at 500 long 'uns according to Wattsy.

It takes a while for all this to sink in. We're just sitting there in silence when Wattsy pipes up again. 'There's only one thing to do in the circumstances, gentlemen,' he says. 'And that's open a book. So who wants a pony on who's going to be the next boss?'

Thursday 18th

Vic put a monkey on Bobby Robson. Friend of a friend of his sat next to the geezer on a plane and he says he told him he was deffo on the way back to England. Wattsy says he's got an insider's nod on Chris Waddle and Bubbles has put a century on a Clough double act, Nigel and Brian. Apparently the lad down his dry-cleaners saw Mr Chairman having lunch with the pair of them out at that swanky hotel near the airport when he was delivering a consignment of table cloths. Or someone who looked like them, anyhow.

Me? I'm sticking a bit closer to home. Yes, that's right. Player-Boss. After all, if Vialli, Lombardo and that bald geezer at Bristol Rovers can do it, Darren Tackle can. I can see lots of advantages in holding down the two jobs: double wages, always sure of a place in the first team, too busy for training, plenty of action on the old pizza commercials front. More you think about it, more it makes sense. I know all the strokes the lads pull when they don't want to train, I know precisely where they all are on Thursday-night curfew, I've been there, done that and put me towel on the sun-lounger before the Germans. Eh, no one will get away with any piss-taking while I'm in charge. In fact, I think I'll get on the mobile to Rodney now. See if he can't fix up a meet with Mr Chairman right away.

Wednesday 24th

My bid to be player-boss hasn't quite got off to the flier I was hoping. Rodney has been completely unavailable and I keep getting that wuss Tristram. He tells me he'll fax Mr Chairman soon as he's back from his Christmas break.

Typical that. I tell you, I can only dream of Christmas breaks. You fans, you think it's easy, don't you, the life of a professional footballer. You think it's all falling out of bed at nine and then larking about with the lads in the fresh air for a couple of hours in the morning, then spending the rest of the day putting in some quality rest. Yeah, but what you don't realise is we have to do that over Christmas.

Now that ten grand a week starts to be put into perspective, dunnit? There's no turkey, no crackers, no brandy butter for Darren Tackle, you know. While the rest of the nation spends their time decorating the bottom of the lamp-posts down River Street in festive minestrone, this particular highly honed athlete is putting in two hours' hard graft on Christmas Eve itself, to set himself up to provide entertainment for you lot on Boxing Day.

Though, as it happens, this morning when we've all turned up about eleven, Wattsy announces out on the training pitch that we're not bothering. You should have seen the look on Old Demo's face. See, with the Boss gone, he's meant to be in charge until a permanent replacement is found.

'But lads, I've got a nice exercise I got from watching the Norwegian darts team prepare,' he says.

'On your own, Demo,' says Wattsy. 'The rest of the gentlemen and me is off for a spot of yuletide revels.'

And like everyone else, Old Demo knows there's no arguing with Wattsy.

Anyhow, just as I'm on me way to the changing-rooms, to stuff me face in one of old Jeanie-from-the-canteen's mega Christmas special lunch balm cakes – turkey, brandy butter and all that biz in a bun – Old Demo calls me over.

'I'm dropping you for Boxing Day, Dazz,' he says. Just like that.

Frankly, I was stunned. Drop me? But I *am* this club.

'What else can I do?' he goes. 'The *People* gave you a three again on Saturday.'

'Come on, Deems,' I says. 'You're not going let a few numbers in the papers tell you who's in and who's out, are you?'

'Now, Dazz. Don't start thinking I'm in any way dictated to by the press,' he says. 'But it's not just the *People*. Did you read Liam McSweeney on Sunday?'

Who?

'You've not heard of McSweeney?'

No.

'I despair. McSweeney is not so much a sportswriter as a poet. Last of the breed. Knows his stuff backwards. Not like these middle-class toe-rags today with their fantasy football and their comedy quiz shows. This, my lad, is what he said about you, and I quote . . .'

At which point he gets a crumpled newspaper cutting out of his tracksuit pocket and starts.

'". . . The best of football players etch their presence on to the national consciousness by employing an astonishing amalgam of natural gifts whose remorseless logic pushes into unfavourable juxtaposition the shadowy interior motives of lesser mortals. Unfortunately Darren Tackle's performance on the shimmering acres of Stamford Bridge yesterday suggests that when the audit of human talent is ultimately completed, his name will not be at the very summit of the register."

'There, Dazz, what do you say to that?'

'Sod-all, Deems,' I says, not following a bleedin' word. 'I'm off to get a Jeanie special.'

Course, when I walk into the canteen, they're all jeering at me. Turns out the soft trout's only made a dozen of them, hasn't she, and they're all gone by the time I get there.

'God, lads,' I says. 'Haven't you saved one for the Dog?'

Then Mickey Scanlan, old Grandad, pipes up that I don't deserve a Jeanie special any road up.

'They're only for first teamers,' he says.

'You what?' I says.

'Word is, you're out for Boxing Day,' he says. 'So, sod off to the bacon rolls with the rest of the stiffs.'

Like I said, you lot have no idea of the sacrifices.

Thursday 25th

One thing about this temporary set-back, only those playing Boxing Day have to go in for training Christmas morning. Everyone else is given a rare morning off. Which is just as well, as the snooker tournament I had with Donald and his mates didn't end till five. Then Donald decided it would be a good crack to open up a bottle of Malibu I got from Nigel the boot rep for Christmas. Course, I had to make sure the sponging get didn't end up with it all, so I've woke up this morning with a concrete head on.

About midday, Donald appears in me bedroom where I am occupying the bed of pain, tells me I've got to get to mam's for Christmas dinner and could I drop him and his mates at their club on the way. I tell him, after the last time, there's no way I'm taking any of my motors anywhere near mam's place. I'll be taxi-ing it, I tells him. He says he's not waiting around for a cab on Christmas Day, he'll make his own way. Typical Donald, that, leaving a geezer on his own when he could do with some company, it being Christmas and that. Particularly as when I rings the cab company I get the usual bollocks we celebs have to put up with.

'Yeah, and I'm Uncle Bulgaria of the Wombles,' the bloke at the other end goes.

'Look,' I says, 'this really is Darren Tackle.'

'Well, if you really are Darren Tackle, tell me this,' he says. 'Why can't you keep your bleedin' legs shut on the goal line?'

Eventually, he says he'll send a cab, but it'll take two hours and if I want one back, it's best to keep the driver on wait and return, seeing as how it's Christmas Day and all. Oh, and it'll cost me £200.

All in all then, I arrives at mam's well late, and with me head ready to crack open, what with me hangover and two hours on the Sony PlayStation I bought meself as a little pre-Christmas comfort gift when I was out stocking up on shirts last week. What with getting in stuff for meself and all the grief about the Boss going, I've not had a moment to do any Christmas shopping. So I've popped a few freebies I've got off me sponsors and that into a holdall. There's a couple of sweat shirts for our Lee and a pair of Ultima Tackles for Donald (not sure of his size, but he can always take them in to AllSports and get a cash refund). For mam there's a box of Deep Heat and a little crate of them plakky bottles of Lucozade. Not much, granted, but it's the thought that counts. And there's sod-all for our Clayton, since he's had £1,100 worth of tasty wheel already off-of me.

Course, when I gets there, there's no sign of our Lee or our Clayton – both out, apparently – and Donald's spark out on the sofa after lunchtime down his club. So the only people there are mam and Hayley, our Lee's bird, who spends the entire time blubbing because she's seventeen, several months up the duff, her old man's kicked her out and her boyfriend's buggered off all day Christmas Day. She was that mithered, not even me offering to autograph her pregnant stomach cheered her up. Mind you, me mam was pretty pleased with the Deep Heat.

'Ooh, pet, how thoughtful,' she says. 'You remembered about me bad back.'

'Oh aye,' I says, pretending like I'd remembered. 'When you've rubbed some on, any chance of popping round my gaff? Donald and his pals had a right session last night, and someone puked Malibu all over me sofa.'

'That was you, you twat,' says Donald, who we all thought was out dead to the world.

Anyhow, not much in the way of festive spirit. After a couple of hours watching *101 Great Green Moments* on the box and listening to Hayley snuffle and Donald snore, there's a ring on the doorbell. It's only the cabbie, innit.

'I just fell asleep in the car,' he says. 'And when I wakes up, all me wheels have been pinched.'

Friday 26th

I ends up kipping in me old bedroom, which is well weird as Mam has turned it into a shrine to yours truly. There's pictures of me with me local team when I was a kid, there's me with a right minging haircut when I made me debut for the Greens, there's tons of trophies and medals lined up in a little display case. I'm just lying there, thinking that I haven't added anything to that display since I was sixteen – well, apart from the Silver Stud, the trophy the fanzine gives the dirtiest player in the club, which I managed to get for one year before it was awarded to Wattsy in perpetuity after that tackle on Zola at Stamford Bridge last year – when the mobile goes. It was Demo.

'Get up,' he says. 'You're in the team this afternoon.'

'Brilliant,' I says. 'S'pose you woke up this morning and realised you couldn't do without the Dog.'

'No,' he says. 'I'm desperate. Half the first team's gone down with bloody food poisoning. The turkey in Jeanie-in-the-canteen's Christmas special baps turned out to be three weeks past its sell-by.'

'Mickey Scanlan one of the sicknotes by any chance?'
I says.

'As it happens, yes,' he says.

Somehow appropriate, this festive time, to learn there
is a God.

Saturday 27th

As I've said before, as a professional, you pay no heed to
what the papers write: build you up to knock you down,
that's their game. Plus always looking for the private-life
angle, as if snorting a pound of coke a night, servicing
the chairman's wife and losing all your money on spread
betting about matches you're involved in has got anything
to do with the way you conduct yourself professionally
speaking. So I've given up reading them. Well, except
this morning.

'DAZZLA DAZZA HAZZA STORMA' was the headline in
the *Sun*. The *Mail* had 'TACKLE STEAMS BACK WITH
WONDER GOAL'. But the best headline was in the *Tele-
graph*: 'RECALLED DARREN TACKLE REPAYS STAND-IN
MANAGER'S FAITH WITH A STUNNING 40-YARD EQUALISER
TO SAVE YULETIDE BLUSHES IN SCRAPPY RELEGATION
BATTLE WATCHED BY A CROWD OF 19,423'. Bit long,
maybe, but at least it saves you having to read the
article.

They have their knockers, don't they, the press men
and the media and that, but Darren Tackle's not one not
to give credit where it's due. So *bona fide* respect to the
lads with inky fingers. And let's hear it for a stonking New
Year for yours truly. Oh yes, a place in Glenn Hoddle's
World Cup squad is within my sights. Just hope he didn't
clock that my forty-yard wonder goal was a hit-and-hope
clearance.

JANUARY

Monday 5th

Yes. Game on. I bell Rodney on the mobile on the way
in to training and, as per usual, he's not there. But that
Tristram, or whatever he's called, has finally got back to
work after spending a festive fortnight comatose in front
of the Christmas Special *Only Fools and Horses*, which is
what I understand you normal people do over the holiday.
And he tells me he's finally faxed Mr Chairman with my
details. Bit delayed maybe, but Darren Tackle's bid for
the managerial vacancy at the Daihatsu is now officially
under way.

   To show that I mean business, I've begun me research.
I've bought Fergie's diaries (not read them obviously, but
they'll look well impressive casually slung over the back
seat of the Jeep when I turns up for the interview). Also
I've watched a couple of episodes of that *Dream Team*
on Sky One to see how they do it. And I've tuned in
to WolfFM when I've been driving in to training and
caught Tommy Docherty spouting off about this, that
and sod-all in particular. No one could deny, then, I'm
putting in the graft.

   Though really, I think there's only a limited amount
yours truly needs to learn about the management game.
My entire career up till now has been like an apprentice-
ship for this: I've watched, and I've listened. Oh aye,
I've listened. The media and that may well have labelled

Darren Tackle the kind of player who never listens to what his coaches have told him. But that shows what they know. I have always listened very careful to what coaches and that have had to say. Then and only then have I told them to fuck off.

Besides, I reckon it's all down to the individual. And I've already worked out a lot of the strategy I'll adopt when I'm gaffer. Basically, you've got to be flexible as a coach in today's modern football, be prepared to mix your styles. So sometimes, in the dug-out, it'll be the suit and the long fancy coat, like your Dalglishes and your Sounesseseses. And other times training gear. But never your Wenger-style track-coat-over-blazer-and-slacks horror show, that is an absolute no-no. Basically a manager, if he wants to win the respect of his players, first and foremost has to have a touchline turn-out like your Ruud Gullits: suede trainers with no socks, beanie hats, that kind of thing, plus a few Calvin Klein tops for the post-match interviews with your Barry Daviesses.

Not, of course, that it did Ruud much good in the long run. But then again, when your Chairman's got third-degree face fungus and he's the sort of bloke what wears a dead bear on his head when the going gets parky down the Bridge, it doesn't matter what kind of sartorial beacon a geezer lights, there's not much hope.

Tuesday 6th

I thought it might not be a bad idea to reinforce the fax by having a face-to-face with Mr Chairman, just see how the land lies. So, I've buzzed over to the stadium after training and I'm hanging around the car-park, trying to keep me head down to avoid any punters coming out of the HumungoStore, hoping to bump into him all casual-like.

Oi, Shearer! £15 million means nothing when you've got Tackle wrapped round your tackle.

As Alex Ferguson has said, a lot of refs are going to be well embarrassed when they see photographic evidence of their decisions. I mean, I got carded for foot-up on this one. Are they blind or what?

Again, clear evidence of victimisation here. A yellow for Tackle while the other geezer, despite dangerous use of the shoulder-blade, gets away with nothing more than a stretcher, an X-ray down the Royal Infirmary and four months in plaster. Where's the justice in that?

I'll give you 6.5 for artistic impression, Nicky.

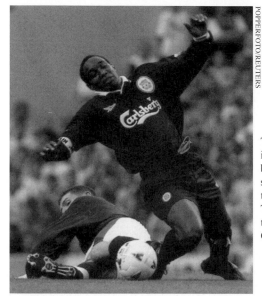

The Guvnor feels the full impact of the Ultima Tackle boot's new SupaBlade™ stud system. Yes, kids, the only way to ensure that you tackle like Tackle is to get your folks to fork out for a pair. Only £169.99 a throw.

The great thing about football is that whatever happens out there on the park, you always share a beer in the bar afterwards. Though on this occasion I seem to remember the geezer chucked his over me head.

Ref, I went for the ball.

Seconds before this slider from Tackle, Stan Collymore sported a full head of hair.

Grace, artistry and skill: the three most over-rated attributes at this level of the game.

It's a man's game out there. Though occasionally you feel the need to hold hands.

My new goal celebration. Oh all right, it's not me, it's Christopher Wreh. See, the photo library didn't have records stretching back far enough to include me scoring a goal. But this is what I would do if I ever scored. Or could do a back-flip.

I'd go to any lengths to meet my idols. And this time Eric Cantona looked pretty pleased to see me, too.

It's only been an hour or so when bingo! He suddenly appears and waltzes straight towards me. I thought I'd just plunge in and tell him about my plans for doing away with club ties on away trips, but then I remember it was the first time I've been one-on-one with him since that white wine business in the Allied Dunbar suite. Probably best to let him say the first word. When he spots me, though, he just starts laughing.

'Darren Tackle, player-manager,' he says, beside himself as he walks past me. 'Darren Tackle, player-manager. That, if I may say so, is an absolute cracker.'

'You what?' I says, extra polite-like.

'You know me, son, not one to beat about the bush,' he says, climbing into his Roller. 'Say what I think, me. As I say, what's on me lung's on me tongue. I'll not spare your feelings with kind words. You, sunshine, have about as much chance of managing this club as I have of getting an invite to Melinda Messenger's for the weekend and being told not to forget to pack the baby oil. Though now I come to think of it, probably slightly less. The only way you will put your backside in the managerial hot seat at the Daihatsu is over my dead body. Right now, from what I've heard, you've enough difficulty holding down a first-team place. Just concentrate on playing for the minute, that's my advice, son. And leave the big decisions to the grown-ups.'

I suppose that's what you call a vote of confidence from the Chairman.

'Nice touch of Chardonnay, that, mind,' he says, easing down his window as he swishes out the car-park. 'Any chance of a couple of bottles for my cellar?'

I think I could just about manage that.

Wednesday 7th

Day three of the campaign sees me arriving early at training, to put to work some of the strategy I've worked out overnight. In all the hoo-ha and speculation, everyone's forgotten that we've got a cup tie on Sunday which could – quite literally – put a bomb under our season. And yours truly has established exactly how we're going to win that one and take the first big step on that Wembley way. I've just drawn me cunning new formation on to the whiteboard when Old Demo walks in.

'Blimey,' he says, seeing me. 'I must still be asleep and dreaming this: Darren Tackle first in training. Pinch me, pinch me, tell me this is not happening.'

Twat.

'Anyhow, what's that you're doodling, Dazz?'

'Not a doodle, Deems,' I says, sounding strangely like a farmyard cockerel. 'It's the way we'll beat those bastards on Sunday and get to Wembley.'

'You what?'

'Right, I see I needs to explain,' I says, thinking here's the chance to show me communication skills. 'You've heard of the Revie W, Ramsey's wingless wonders and Terry V's Christmas tree?'

'Yeah.'

'Well this is Darren's Doughnut.'

'You what?'

'Basically, as I say, it's a formation like a wheel, with one player in the middle and everyone else running round him, doing, like, all the work. All the play goes through the geezer in the middle. He's what you call the wossname. You know the, erm, wossitcalled.'

'Fulcrum?'

'No need to be rude, Deems,' I says. 'No, the bit in the middle of the wheel. Anyhow, that's how we'll win Sunday, with Darren's Doughnut.'

'So who is the geezer in the middle?' says Demo. 'Carmine?'

'No.'

'Bubbles?'

'No.'

'Wattsy, then.'

'No.'

'Vic? Bob? Mickey Scanlan?'

'No it's not knobbin' Mickey Scanlan,' I says, thinking it's no wonder Demo's never going to get far in football when he can't see the bleedin' obvious when it's staring him in the face. 'It's me. I'm the geezer what invented the system, so I'm the geezer what gets to play in the best position.'

'You? Play-maker?' says Demo, looking like I've just asked to borrow a long 'un off-of him. 'Just shut it, Dazz, and get a bib on.'

Yeah, best get your scoffing in now, Demo. Because you'll be laughing all the way to the dole queue when I'm player-manager.

Thursday 8th

Get a call on the mobile on the way into training from some right posho.

'Is that Mr Tackle?'

'Might be.'

'Mr *Darren* Tackle?' says the voice, making out like Darren's another word for dog crap or summat.

'Yeah, and who the hell are you when you're at home?'

'My name's Miller. Of Miller & Arafat.'

'And . . .'

'Miller & Arafat, Aston Martin dealers in Mayfair. Your DB7, sir, is ready for collection.'

'Shite, I'd clean forgot the bastard.'

'As I feared, sir.'

'You what?'

'Indeed,' the geezer sighs. 'What arrangements would you care to make for its collection, sir?'

'Just get one of your blokes to drop it round my place. But for Christ's sake, make sure it's in the afternoon, when I'm in.'

Last thing I need, see, is Donald getting his mitts on it.

'We don't deliver, sir,' the geezer goes. 'Insurance premiums preclude such a service. So would sir care to make himself an appointment to collect the car, perhaps?'

Knob it. Ninety long 'uns and I have to make an appointment to drive down the smoke to collect. I don't suppose Rodney would be in if I rang to get him to sort it, there's no way I'm letting that Tristram or whatever he's called anywhere near me upholstery, so I suppose I'll have to do it meself. The sacrifices I make.

Friday 9th

According to speculation in this morning's papers, the Greens are about to join the continental shuffle and appoint a foreign manager. Apparently, Mr Chairman is trying to buy out the contract of some Latvian geezer who's currently coaching in Istanbul. Until he arrives, Demo will carry on in temporary charge, with Old Grandad, Mickey Scanlan, as player-coach. Surely not Grandad. Not even Mr Chairman would make that kind of mistake. I mean, what sort of image of the club is Grandad going to present? If you said Tommy Hilfiger to him he'd ask you if he was Grimsby's left-back. If you're going to go for someone what's ga-ga, you might as well go the whole hog and get in Bobby Robson. Though Wattsy tells me it's cast-iron that Robson's off to Goodison. Remember, he once got the heave-ho out of Barcelona when they ended up runners-up? Apparently reckons he'll be well safe at Everton; no chance of ever coming anywhere near second there.

Me, I'm still hopeful I can make Mr Chairman see sense and appoint the right man for the job. Though I have to say, this morning didn't exactly help my cause. For the first time in about six months, the man himself turns up at training, showing a couple of blokes with tape measures and clipboards round the new facilities. If, as I suspect, he's there to once-over a couple of candidates for the managerial post, then his timing couldn't have been worse.

In the middle of the training pitch, Demo's droning on and on about some routine developing the muscle tension on the back of the achilles to help improve explosive pace or summat. And there's only Grandad and the foreign lads paying any attention. Me, Wattsy, Vic, Bob, Bubbles and that lot is rehearsing our new formation goal celebration ready for the big cup-tie on Sky on Sunday. According to Wattsy, who made it up, it's 'an homage to *Hawaii Five-O*' and it involves six of us doing synchronised belly-flops into the corner. We'd just tried it for the fifth time when I spots Mr Chairman over by the new block. Just hope he didn't clock it was me standing on the backs of the prostrate figures of Vic and Bob, singing 'did-a-did-a-dee-dee, did-a-did-a-dee' at the top of me voice while paddling like I'm that Redgrave bloke on the last 50 metres of the Olympic gold-medal run.

Monday 12th

It's not always easy to look on the bright side. Especially when, as a pro, you're out to give of your best in each and every situation. And this was about as low as things can sink. But I can't help just the merest little smile inside when I thinks about Demo and Old Grandad's chances of landing the manager's job permanent after the right bollocks they made of yesterday's game.

First off, Demo drops me. Again. Which in normal circumstances is a complete no-no. But this turns out to be the sort of game where it's a case of them what's missing can't be held to blame. Besides, top thing about a Sky game, they have a camera placed right by the bench, so you get your mug on the box constant, and if I look interested and that, Mr Chairman might well note the credentials.

As for the game, it all goes wrong for us after Carmine's knocked an early goal in. When he's scored, he's pulled his shirt over his head as is his usual way and has dived full-length towards the corner flag, where he's lain expecting the other lads to dive in and mob him. After about a minute, he's started to get that lonely feeling. He's pulled the shirt off his head and noticed there's no one near him, everyone's standing round the centre circle, looking a bit embarrassed, waiting to kick off. Because he was off doing his own thing at training, obviously he can't have heard Wattsy's clear instruction that when we got a goal, everyone should do the 'Hawaii Five-O'. Unless Carmine scores. In which case, here's a chance to show the rest of the country what we think of him, and he's to be completely ignored.

Anyhow, though I couldn't stop pissing meself on the bench at the sight of Carmine just lying there, waiting to be mobbed, and all the other lads just walking back to get on with it, he didn't see the funny side. Specially when the ref yellowed him for excessive celebration.

Looking back on it, Wattsy and the lads might agree that showing him up like that may not have been the best tactic in a full-blooded cup tie. Geezer goes into a sulk and doesn't kick a ball for the rest of the match, spending his time moping around, moaning about lack of service. Meanwhile, the oppo put five away, making Demo's preparations look bollocks and leaving Grandad heaving round the centre circle like he's got a virulent case of BSE and can no longer walk in a straight line. Me, I only got the last fifteen minutes, replacing our sulky Paraguayan, who, incidentally, goes straight off out of it without even bothering to shower never mind shake me by the hand. Quarter of an hour: it was never enough time for time to effect any change. All I could do is watch as three of their goals go in. On for such a short outing, the papers didn't think it was worth giving me a mark. Leastwise, I expect that's why the *Sun* popped a nought next to me name.

Tuesday 13th

Bottom of the league, out the Coca-Cola, out the FA, no manager and with a half-wit and his no-clue side-kick in temporary charge, this is a club on the sick-list. We are going down.

Still, it's not all doom and gloom: Wattsy's going to give us a lift down to London to pick up the new engine.

After training we get threaded up for a trip to the smoke. I've got a new Armani ski jacket in primrose, with Nicole Farhi flares in stretch and a pair of Timberlands customised by R. Soles of River Street with a four-inch heel. And Wattsy's in an all-in-one Versace leather jogging suit, with a pair of Gucci loafers in chocolate. Since we don't want to be mithered, we've both got Aviator shades on. All I can say is, I just hope them cockney lasses is all carrying a spare pair of knickers. 'Cos they'll all be wetting the ones they've got on when they spies the two of us driving into their town.

Anyhow, we're just spinning off down the ring-road in Wattsy's white Merc E36 with full AMG body kit, eighteen-inch radials, tinted windows – tasty wheels, Wattsy's, gets you noticed, that sort of set – when we gets pulled over by a couple of dibble on motorbikes. Here we go, I thinks, the usual.

'All right, Sambo,' says the first copper as Wattsy purrs down the window. 'What's your drop today? Charlie or E? Or is the big rasta man moving up in the world to a little H?'

He's had some, Wattsy. So like the all-round top-class pro he is, he shows his experience and, without a word, he's handed over his driving licence with a pair for the Liverpool game carefully folded into it.

'My apologies, Mr Watts, for not immediately recognising you,' says the copper, when he's read the licence and popped the tickets into his tunic as if nothing has happened. 'Oh, and I see you've got Mr Tackle in there with you.'

'All right, Wattsy?' goes the other copper, leaning into the motor. 'All right, Dazz? How's the barnet?'

'I'm glad we've run into you two officers,' Wattsy goes. 'We're in a bit of a hurry, we could use an escort down to the Smoke.'

'If you could get us into the Allied Dunbar for the match, we'll see you down there no problem, Mr Watts, sir,' says the first Dibble.

'What,' says Wattsy, 'with pre-match dining facilities, at-seat hostess service and the opportunity after the game for a guided tour of the new club museum accompanied by a former player?'

'Yup,' says the second dibble.

'Consider it done, officers,' says Wattsy.

So all in all we're down in London in double-quick time.

But when we walks into Miller & Arafat, there's about ten sales fellas standing around and all of them looks at the pair of us like we've never heard of the term personal hygiene.

'Back door, lads,' says one geezer. And he must have noticed I'm about to chin him for bleedin' cheek, because he adds, pointing with his thumb over his shoulder as he speaks: 'Deliveries go round the back, chaps.'

'I'm not here to deliver,' I says, well cheesed off by now. 'I'm here to take away.'

'Oh, you mean the waste paper,' says the bloke. 'I think you'll find that's still round the back.'

'Not waste paper,' I goes. 'A DB7.'

When the penny finally drops and geezer shows us to the car, he sticks his nose so far in the air, I'm surprised it's not got snow on it. But so what, this is one slick prick of an engine. And I've got one and he hasn't. It's smooth, smart and in a delicate shade of Acapulco Gold which will turn heads by the dozen down River Street of a Saturday night. Best of all, Wattsy tells me on the way down that he's read in *Auto Trader* that the waiting list for these bastards is now so bleedin' long that if I sell it tomorrow, I should be able to pull at least fifteen long 'uns profit.

'I'll just arrange for the front doors to be opened and the car driven on to the street,' says the geezer, as Wattsy and me check out whether you can see your own reflection in the paintwork. 'In the meantime, would you mind signing the release forms? Or at least putting your mark on them.'

I've just popped me moniker on his papers (and in the process added about three long 'uns to their value), when it occurs to me Arafat & Miller theirselves might well be interested in doing an immediate buy-back. You know, do a deal. They could give me a hundred long 'uns here and now, I'd slip in a couple of signed photos and an official Greens' lunchbox for goodwill and then I'd go home with Wattsy, ten up for an afternoon's work. Not quite up there in the money-for-old-rope stakes with Paul Gascoigne's fee for a testimonial, but sweet little deal, eh?

'Sir, may I draw your attention to these forms,' says the geezer, after he's heard my very generous offer. 'In order to protect the value of our marque and legislate against rogue profiteering, we insist purchasers sign an undertaking not to re-sell their vehicle for twelve calendar months. Anyone defaulting on the agreement is obliged to refund to us any profit derived from early sale.'

'And?' I says.

'And, sir, you've just signed the agreement.'

Knob. A year.

'By the way, has sir ever driven an Aston before?'

'Nah,' I says. 'But an engine's an engine. Just give us the keys, matey, and I'm off.'

'As sir wishes,' he says. 'But I would advise . . .'

'Keys, Prince Charles,' I says.

As Wattsy says as I takes possession of the beast, some draw this'll be, cruising at 110 round the ring-road, cutting up Beamers. And I can't help noticing, as I ease north out of London, and begin to contemplate putting me foot to the floor, heads spinning in my direction. Female heads, I might add. Darren Tackle, you are now in possession of a major-league fanny magnet. If only I could get a handle on this gear change.

Wednesday 14th

Car wouldn't start this morning. Took me twenty minutes to get Donald out of bed to give us a jump start off-of the Jeep. Then when I finally gets off, I gets immediately stuck in one mother of a traffic jam on the gyratory system up by the leisure centre. Last thing I needed is that Tristram or whatever he calls himself ringing on the mobile, just as a little plume of smoke starts coming out the bonnet.

'What?' I says.

'Ah, I see Mr T has got his tetchy head on this morning,' he says.

'Knob it. Not you,' I says.

'Perhaps,' he says, 'Mr T might like Tristram to pop round and take him in hand.'

No I bleedin' wouldn't, I says, as a horrible gurgling noise begins to be heard from up front.

And it's not even as if he's got any worthwhile news, this Tristram. He's on to tell me that some posh Sunday newspaper is looking for an interview tomorrow dinnertime about the disastrous situation at the Daihatsu and what is to be done about it. I ask what the fee is. He says posh papers don't pay for interviews. I tell him to behave. I've just picked up ninety long 'uns' worth of over-heating bleedin' engine which I won't be able to off-load for a year and the one bit of endorsement work he's come up with in months he expects me to do for bobbins.

'Where is bleedin' Rodney?' I says. Not, I might add, for the first time these past few weeks. 'He'll sort this. He knows the rules: a long 'un absolute minimum for any chat with the hyenas.'

'Mr Gee's out, Mr T,' Tristram says. 'But I'm sure he'd fully endorse my recommendations on this one.'

And off he goes with all this about how it would be

good for my image to be seen as a thinker, you know, mature, join the new class of broadsheet footballer, he says. Show Mr Chairman I mean business. Kick-start me campaign to get the player-manager's job. All the usual bollocks.

But I'm having none of it. I says to him I've got some important zeds to catch up on tomorrow. And to be honest, I am beginning to feel a bit of jip in the lower back, so I might have to pay a visit to the lovely Suzette. Whatever, no way am I holing myself up for an hour with some style-free wassock in an anorak with an unhealthy obsession with football. You know, haven't these people got lives to lead? He says it's a shame, because it would be interesting to find out if this new breed of young girl sports reporter know their stuff.

Friday 16th

We meet up at that flash new restaurant built in a converted warehouse in town called Pie & Mighty. It was Wattsy's idea. He'd been to the opening a couple of months back and said it was happening. He'd seen that fat bloke who used to be in Take That there, a bird who'd got her kit off in *FHM* magazine and that barmaid from *Emmerdale* what's just been gang-raped down the Woolpack, an incident what kick-started a campaign in the *Sun* for the rapists to be publicly castrated. Well happening.

It's on about eight different floors, real ultra-modern decor, everything painted lime green, floors, ceilings, doors, the lot. Including these weird designer chairs that are about as comfortable as sitting on a beer crate and are doing my back no good whatsoever. Still, our table's got a great view out over the canal. Plus, by a lucky coincidence, I could keep an eye on the Aston, which was still standing more or less intact where I abandoned it yesterday on the way to training.

'Which one is it?' the bird reporter says, looking out the window across to where the Aston's parked, just next to a Range Rover with a smashed near-side passenger window. The very same window through which, as I'm pointing it out, a bloke what looks uncannily like our Clayton is inserting his arm.

'Ah, I see it,' she says. 'The snot-coloured one.'

'Acapulco Gold actually.'

'Oh,' she says. 'I'm not really up to speed on cars. But I interviewed Jurgen Klinsmann once and he's got this lovely little old-fashioned Beetle.'

Not what you'd call a cracker, this one. But still, with a bit of work, I reckon we could get on the same wave-length. When I tell her, for instance – off the record, obviously – the real reason the Boss got the heave-ho she's that impressed, she checks three times that her tape recorder's working properly. And when I fill her in about Carmine's nocturnal habits, she's almost choked on her olive bread. As I say, perhaps not the best-looking bit of skirt this side of Ann Widdecombe, but a couple of lunchtime lagers should soften my critical faculties.

But then the menu arrives.

I've never seen anything like it in my life.

'Ooh, this looks very enterprising,' she says. 'What are you going to have, Darren?'

Well, I'm flummoxed. What the hell is 'Sweetbread compote with red onion marmalade' when it's at home? Or how about 'Beijing crispy squab stuffed with cranberry forcemeat and wrapped in a marjoram brioche?' I'm clue-less, so I pop to the gents to see if I can find another punter who can tell me what to order. I walk in and all there is in the toilet, which is also painted entirely lime green, are these two trough things along either wall, with these little pipes sticking out and mirrors behind them. No sit-downs, basins, towels, three-ply silk-wipe, nothing. As I say, real trendy. There's no one in there, so I take the opportunity to relieve myself. And who should walk in as I'm doing it but Mr Chairman himself.

'Well, knock me down with a lead balloon, it's Darren "Book 'em Danno" Tackle. Never expected to see you in a place as sophisticated as this. By the way,' he says, opening this door in the back wall what I hadn't seen as I walked in, 'what are you doing having a slash in the sink? The lavvies are through this door here.'

Monday 19th

The Aston has yet to be delivered back by the AA. Bloke rung me on the mobile when we was on the way to Coventry for the game on Saturday saying there was too much work to be done and he'd have to tow it into a specialist garage. He said that the gear-box had been burnt out. He said it was terrible what damage these joy-riders can do to expensive motors. I says I didn't think it had been nicked, unless whoever done it had returned it exactly to the spot I'd left it when it over-heated the other day. He said whoever it was had been driving it was a right arsehole, and had clearly got no respect for a fine piece of engineering, because they'd completely buggered up the clutch. Which shows what he knows, because mine's an automatic. I'm certain it is. And if it's not, it ought to be. I mean if you're paying ninety long 'uns for a motor, least the thing can do for you is change gear.

Anyhow, whatever the cause, it means I'm without the car to make a big splash at this evening's Brit awards. Oh, didn't I mention it? Yeah, me, I'm off to the Brits. Football, after all, is the new rock and roll, as my agent

Rodney always says. In fact, it was thanks to Rodders I'm off there.

I got a call this morning from that Tristram saying Rodds had taken a table with some of his old record company friends from the days when he was in the biz and he'd invited Les Ferdinand, but Les had had to drop out at the last minute.

'So I'm first reserve to go instead, then, am I?' I says, sounding not a little peeved.

'Well, not exactly first,' says Tristram. 'But Ian Wright wasn't available, David Beckham was making his own arrangements, and Martin Keown wasn't interested.'

Fantastic to know where I stand in the pecking order, behind Martin Keown.

'So what's the story, dosh-wise?' I says.

'Two hundred and fifty,' says Tristram.

'Is that all?' I says, thinking of big Aston Martin bills that lie up ahead.

'Oh good, Mr Gee didn't think you'd mind,' he says. 'And he says you can owe him, he'll knock it off your next royalty statement.'

Tuesday 20th

Top night, as it happens. Even though Rodders doesn't show. Tristram bells me on the mobile while I'm on me way down to the Smoke to tell me he won't be there.

'Out getting the work for me, I expect,' I says.

'Not exactly,' Tristram says. 'Let's just say there's one or two faces he doesn't need to run into at this particular juncture.'

This Tristram then proceeds to give us a little pep talk about how this is a big opportunity, image-wise. About how Jamie Redknapp's got his Louise, Becksy's got his

Posh and Stan Collymore's got hold of his Ulrika's, and how mixing in the right company is vital for the modern professional. About how getting a snap with that bloke from the 'Bizarre' column in the *Sun* with his arm round me like we're big mates is worth plenty in add-ons to the bottom line.

'And Darren,' he finishes, 'ration the sauce.'

Bleedin' nerve. Besides, I don't need to worry about the booze: there's a free bar. Soon as I walks in, I gets straight over there, thinking that's where Liam and Noel will be hanging out. I was looking forward to rubbing shoulders with them, preferably in the gents, while leaning over the cistern.

As it happens, they're not there either. But it's a star-studded event all right. I see Lennox Lewis, the goofy bloke in shades what wrote 'Three Lions', plus that bird off-of *Live and Kicking*. Oh, and Steve McManaman is there representing the Liverpool hombres, who like to think of theirselves as the coolest dudes in football, but frankly aren't a patch on me, Wattsy and that lot in the fashion stakes. I lets on to Macca, but he doesn't seem to recognise me out of me kit.

The best thing is, though, I'm standing at the bar talking to this bloke what says he used to be the drummer from Hawkwind, when the photographer from the *Sun* turns up with that Scary from the Spice Girls and only asks me to pose with me arms round her. I tell you, she's 110 per cent woman Scary, there's bits of her all over the shop, and I gets a nice little tongue injection in on her as we're doing the pictures.

I've not told the lads yet. I've just said look out for the papers on Wednesday.

Wednesday 21st

I goes into training, cock of the walk, and they're all there in the dressing-room, gathered round a couple of copies of the *Sun*. Yeah, I think, top this, Wattsy.

'La-di-da, it's the Dog,' says Wattsy as I walks in. 'We're just enjoying page twelve of this morning's edition of that esteemed organ, the *Sun*.'

And he chucks over his copy. I turns to the 'Bizarre' column and there, sure enough, is a picture of me and Scary giving it plenty.

'Every Dog has his day,' I grins.

'Oh aye, Dog, indeed they do,' says Wattsy, and by now, everyone's pissing themselves. 'May I suggest you actually read the caption.'

Just as I'm about to read it, who should walk in but Mr Chairman.

'Ah, Tackle,' he says. 'Reading up on your exploits, I see. I've already read the paper and I must say I'm thrilled to see your campaign to be taken seriously in this club is off to such a flier.'

And he's off out, with everyone giving it a chorus of 'wooos' and 'waaahs' in my direction once he's gone.

'You're just bleedin' jealous,' I says. Then I reads the paper.

'Stop right now,' it reads. 'My Spice Girls lookalikes were so realistic, they even fooled top Premiership star Darren Tackle. Here's my Scary-alike and Dazza looking as if they wannabe alone. Mind you, Dazza had been enjoying the awards hospitality so much I don't suppose he'd have noticed if he'd ended up kissing the Greens' club mascot Fi-Fi the Flounder.'

All in all, he's probably right, Mr Chairman: I think I'll concentrate on the playing side just now.

FEBRUARY

Monday 2nd

Skipped training this morning. To be honest, my lower back's giving me all sorts of jip, not helped by Saturday's farce, when Demo made me the sacrificial lamb and I was dropped for the Liverpool game. Bleedin' thoughtless of the old fool and all, making a man in my condition sit on the bench throughout. As a result of ninety minutes sat on a backless board getting splinters up me arse, even the lovely Suzette can't loosen us up down there. In fact I stiffen up just at the thought of her probing Gallic fingers.

Besides, the bloke from the garage said the Aston's being returned today, and there's no way I'm risking Donald taking delivery. Not that I feel remotely guilty about having a little kip this morning instead of tearing round the training field like some YTS-keenie on an arse-wipe exercise of Demo's. As Alex Ferguson has pointed out, preserving energy is so vital at this point of the season that forty winks is probably the best preparation a pro can have for a big game. Though forty might be pushing the wink rate, given the noise Donald and his pals is making putting the tiles back up in the kitchen where they all fell off last week under the weight of plaster on the adjoining conservatory wall. Still, a few lagers in front of Richard and Judy should send me off efficiently to the land of nod.

Tuesday 3rd

Sod it. I went out like a light at precisely the wrong moment. I'm woken up by this bloody great big crash which I assume at first to be Donald falling off his step-ladder, but then I realise has come from outside. I leg it out as fast as my dodgy back will allow into the garden, where I am confronted with a scene of devastation. There is no other word for it. It's quite literally like downtown Baghdad after a visit from one of them smart bombs out there. Me back garden is transformed into a morass of splintered glass and twisted bits of concrete and steel. A snow-drift of plaster dust has settled on me lawn. And there, in the middle of me conservatory, is the Aston with Donald slowly climbing out the driver's seat.

'Knob!' I screams. 'What have you done this time, Donald?'

Turns out me worst nightmare has indeed come true. While I'm zedding as Richard and Judy discuss the male menopause on their sofas with Christopher Biggins, the Aston has been returned. Seems Donald, thinking he's doing me a favour not waking me, decides he's going to put it into the garage. He slots it into reverse and starts to back it up. But he has under-estimated the sheer animal power of this machine and is going too fast. So he aims to slam his foot on the brake, he says. Typical: instead, he puts his foot on the accelerator. And he sends it, all two ton of hand-tooled motoring excellence, flying through the back wall of the garage across the lawn and into the conservatory, finally coming to a halt so close to the snooker table that if you wanted to do a double off the cushion into the top left-hand pocket, you'd be best attempting it from the back seat of the car.

I'm standing there, completely, as I say, gob-smacked, while Donald emerges from a motor which looks like it won't be driven for a while.

'Tell you what, lad,' is all he says as he stands there, doubled up like an old man. 'You ought to get that driving position looked at. It doesn't half give you jip in the back.'

Wednesday 4th

Couldn't wait to get off to training this morning, what with the state me gaff's in. I've left Donald and his pals to get on with the clear-up, which, he says, he was too shocked to do anything about yesterday.

'Lucky I'm on hand,' he says to me, standing there at the front door wrapped in the terry towelling dressing-gown with the club crest which I believe once happened to be mine. 'I tell you what, lad, I'll do you a very decent quote on a re-build for the conservatory and all while I'm about it.'

When I gets to training the car-park is awash with media and that. There's television cameras, there's photographers, there's radio men and they all surrounds me as I climb – gingerly, I have to say – out the Jeep which I am having to drive for reasons too bleedin' obvious to state here.

'Any comment, Dazz?' they all go.

'To be honest, I'm not comfortable at all in meself,' I says. 'Obviously as a pro I want to give 110 per cent. But at the moment, with this back, I'm feeling as how I can only deliver 98, maybe 99 per cent at the absolute outside.'

'Not your back,' says one of them. 'Have you got any comments about the New Gaffer. He arrives today, and you were, after all, regarded in some quarters as being in with a chance of landing the job yourself. So how do you feel? Are you happy about the appointment? Any resentment at all?'

To be honest, what with all the reconstruction going on at my place, I'd clean forgot he was arriving today. So I give it the usual response.

'I'm well looking forward to meeting the New Gaffer and working with him. I'm sure I speak for the rest of the lads when I say we'll all be giving him our full backing and putting in the graft necessary to make sure we're all playing Premiership football next season.'

Which means, if results carry on they way they are doing, getting our agents on their blowers pronto to sort us all out with transfers over the summer.

When I walks into the changing-room, instead of getting bibbed up and that for training, Old Demo tells us all to report to the gym. And while we're all standing around, enjoying the sort of laugh you have as a bunch of lads (Bob's got a new pair of shoes, good enough excuse in my book for a bit of light-hearted banter along the lines of, 'Them's shite shoes, Bob, what the fuck did you buy them for?'), he walks in. Here he is at last: the New Gaffer.

I'd seen him on the telly, obviously, but in the flesh he's a bit of a surprise. Can't say he looks like a football manager for a start. More like a teacher. In fact, he reminds me of that git we had for technology at my old place, all bottle-bottomed specs and leather elbow patches. He was the geezer what got our Clayton excluded. And all the lad had done was engage in a bit of boisterous horse-play involving the lathe in the metalwork department. All right, so the teacher needed forty-two stitches in a head wound and was pensioned off soon after, suffering from a chronic nervous disorder, but there was no need to over-react.

Anyhow, Old Demo introduces us all to the New Gaffer one by one.

'Ah, Darren Tackle,' he says when he reaches me. 'Your notoriety precedes you.'

Ta very much. I'll take that as a compliment and all.

When he's met everyone, he makes a little speech. And fair play to the fella, turns out he speaks pretty handy English for a Latvian. Which is more than can be said for half our dressing-room at the moment. I suppose Carmine gets by all right – enough to let us all know his contempt any road – but the Bosnian lads are clueless. I asked one of them the other week if he'd copped for any English totty yet and how did it compare to the snatch in downtown Sarajevo, and he flew into a right egg and went off bleating to his mates. Thought I'd asked him to make me a cup of tea, it seems.

I reckon if you're foreign and that and you're coming over here, you'd think you'd try to learn the lingo. I mean, Incey and Gazza and that lot, when they went to Italy, everyone there made an effort and spoke English to them, didn't they? So if everyone could speak English in Italy, it's only right they should try and do it here and all.

Trouble is, as Wattsy said, the moment he started, the New Gaffer might speak perfect English but you need an interpreter to understand a bleedin' word he says. No dropping in the hole, putting it in the mixer or getting a lead on early doors for him. It's all diametrics and re-establishment of gain lines and stuff. He wants to re-prioritise our approach to the final third.

Still, one thing I followed, he says he isn't here to do a clear-out. He won't pre-judge nobody, he says, everyone will be given the chance to impress him over the next few months.

'And together,' he says, 'if we apply our intelligence collectively to the dilemma we face, we will emerge victorious on the far bank of our own individual Rubicon.'

'Rubicon?' Wattsy whispers to me. 'What's that when it's at home, then? That new curry house down River Street?'

Just one thing, though. The New Gaffer wants to give us all new squad numbers. Afterwards, Bob reckons it was something to do with the commercial department wanting to make sure all the in-breds what fill out the HumungoStore of a Saturday have to dish out for new shirts three months after they bought the last lot. Whatever: Wattsy's gone from 4 to 17, Vic from 8 to 19 and Bob from 11 to 21. And from now on Darren Tackle is number 73.

Thursday 5th

Me back is now so completely seized up, I had to pass meself unfit for last night's game, the New Gaffer's first in charge.

'Tragic news, Gaffer,' I says when I broke it to him.

'No, Darren. This is not tragedy,' he says. 'War, pestilence, famine: those are tragedies. A small child, innocent and gentle, cut down with all its life ahead of it by a driver who has consumed more alcohol than any one system can process: this is tragedy. Darren Tackle missing football match: this is not tragedy. If nothing else, because I play team my esteemed staff picked for Saturday, so you would not be playing anyway. Sit by me on bench and observe. We shall learn together, Darren, you and I.'

Sod me, the geezer's swallowed a poetry anthology.

Ten minutes into the game, and I begin to wonder if Mr Chairman's not made one hell of a ricket bringing this geezer in. We go one down and he don't seem to care. I mean, he doesn't stand up. He doesn't bawl. He doesn't even swear.

'Regroup behind the gain line,' is all he says.

Me, I'm up on me feet, yelling suggestions at Gary Ball, whose taken my slot.

'Bollocks, Bollocks, fuckenell, Bollocks,' I shouts at Ballsy. You know, that kind of tactical help.

'Eh? Fucken do 'em. Bollocks, do 'em, Bollocks, do 'em,' I'm shouting.

And the New Gaffer pulls me down with a little tug on the tracksuit.

'Darren,' he says, 'this is not conducive to improving Gary's performance.'

Well, I tells him, it may not improve Bollocks, but as a professional, I just can't sit there without kicking every ball. You know, it's hard to explain to an ordinary person, the frustration of being on the bench. I just got to, kind of, let it out, you know.

'Have patience, Darren my friend,' he says. 'You must learn to relax. You are too stressed.'

Which isn't something you could accuse him of being. We go into half-time 3–0 down and he doesn't even raise his voice. There's no screaming, no shouting, the dressing-room crockery is safe in this geezer's hands. Instead he goes through each player on the team and carefully tells them what's gone wrong and how they can improve for the second half.

'Gary,' he says to Bollocks, 'your opposite number is occupying too much space. He consumes it like starving man let loose in chocolate factory. You must fill that space yourself. Swell into it. Like balloon, you must inflate into that space, feel yourself filling that space. Come, breathe with me. In. Out. That's it, Gary. Imagine you are balloon.'

'Yeah,' I shouts as Bollocks and the New Gaffer stand there heavy breathing like a pair of dirty old men in a phone box. 'Fucken do the knob, Bollocks.'

'Thank you, Darren,' the New Gaffer says. 'Perhaps you will allow me.'

So I do. And we end up losing 5–0.

Friday 6th

It was Wattsy who suggested it. At first I thought it was your typical Wattsy wind-up. He slips a piece of paper into me hand with a name and number written on it after training. Well, I say training, but I was on the physio's table, as per usual, with the lovely Suzette sending me straight to planet pain every time she puts her fingers anywhere near the dodgy spot on me spine.

'Try it,' he says.

'What?' I says.

'The number on the paper,' he says. 'If anyone can get the Dog back on four legs again, it's Irma.'

'Irma?' I says.

'Yes, Irma Smegova. Faith healer to the footballing fraternity.'

'Knob it, Wattsy, this is no joking matter, me back.'

'Straight up, try it.'

Now I come to think of it, he's had some, Wattsy. Injuries and that. Knuckles out of alignment at Stoke in the Coca-Cola two years ago, bad bruising to his forehead when he unluckily came into contact with that geezer's nose at Tottenham, buggered up his toe against Giggsy's shin at Man U. But when he goes down, he always seems to come through quick.

'Try it, Dog,' he says. 'What you got to lose?'

Nah. Nah. Sorry. It's a wind-up for deffo.

Sunday 8th

Embarrassingly enough, the geezer loading a trolley of ready-mix concrete into the back of his Mondeo had a point.

'This, I cannot believe: Darren Tackle, Premiership

superstar, down B&Q with us ordinary mortals of a Sunday morning. What's occurring here then?'

Dell's, Toff's, Brown's in London when we've got an away in the Smoke, this is the natural habitat of this particular modern-day footballer. Not B&Q of a Sunday morning. But then, most modern-day footballers aren't saddled with bleedin' Donald. See, he said he'd borrow the Jeep to go down and collect some wall panels for the conservatory and before I know what I've said, I've told him no way is he driving any of my engines after the Aston business. So I've gone and said I'll fetch him down there. Problem is, I've popped on a beanie hat and Aviators for a bit of the old incognito and of course, since it's pissing it down with rain, I've stuck out like Mark Hughes's arse. Before I know it, before we've even got past the mahogany toilet seat display, I've got a line of in-breds queueing up for me autograph.

'You had a new hairdo, Dazz?' says one geezer.

'No, why?' I says.

'Just wondered why you had the hat pulled round your ears.'

No disrespect, but some of these punters are right twats. Plus me mood is not greatly chuffed up by the fact that it's me what has to foot the rebuilding bill. Work that one out: Donald smashes my engine through my garage wall and lands in my conservatory, and who is it hefting out for treble thickness glazing panels with riven steel frame? Yo, right first time.

But the final egg on a totally shite morning is when we're loading said panels on to the roof of me Jeep and ping. I feel it going, just like that. Me back, finally done for. I'm doubled up in pain, and Donald has to fold me like a deck chair into the boot. Plus I could have done without the grin on his face when I chucks him the keys to drive us home and all. And it certainly didn't improve me mood, I tell you, when, first time Donald took a corner, the three new conservatory panels slides off and splatters all over the mini-roundabout just outside Pet World.

'Sorry, lad,' he says, climbing out the Jeep to inspect yet more bleedin' Donald damage. 'What with your back going like that and all, I clean forgot to tie them on up there. Shall we pop back and get some more?'

'No we knobbin' won't.'

Monday 9th

Wattsy, seeing me walk into training doubled-up like I've had a heavy night on the vindaloo, is straight over.

'Where is the Dog off to?' he says.

'Physio's,' is about all I can say.

'Irma,' he says. 'I've told you, Irma.'

And before I realise what he's doing, he's fiddled around in me tracksuit pocket, pulled out me mobile and dialled her up.

'Trust me,' he says, handing the mobile over. 'Irma's never failed yet.'

Tuesday 10th

I've tried everything, pills, exercises, the lovely Suzette has virtually set up home in the small of my back, but nothing's worked. And for a footballer, nothing and I mean nothing is worse than not being able to play football. Well, possibly having your skin peeled off and then being rolled in a vat of Marmite might be worse. But ten days out, ten days not kicking a ball and the frustration's almost killing me. Specially as now's the time everyone's jockeying around to impress the New

Gaffer. To be honest, Wattsy's right. What have I got to lose with this Irma?

So I'm off to see her. Obviously, as a professional footballer, you don't travel alone. Besides, state I'm in, there's no way I could drive there. And Wattsy, top man that he is, says he'll do the honours. Trouble is, when he turns up at my house and I waddle out to his motor, who's already in there but Vic and Bob.

'Knob it, Wattsy,' I says. 'You're taking the piss, incha. Sending me off to see some quack faith healer and bringing an audience along to slaughter us.'

'Would I do that, my canine friend?' he says, as I fold meself into the front seat of his Merc. 'Seeing as how Irma lives in Blackpool, Victor and Robert here have just decided to come along for the road trip.'

Oh aye, that's why the pair of them can hardly talk for pissing theirselves.

Turns out this Irma lives in one of them roads behind the prom, endless red-brick semis with net curtains and signs in the window offering B&B for a fiver a night.

It was round here somewhere that mam took us on the only holiday we ever had as kids. I remember like it were yesterday, ten quid was all it cost for a week's accommodation. We had to share a room, mind, the four of us, our Lee got eaten alive by bed bugs and we was kicked out after three nights when our Clayton nicked the ballcock out the cistern in the shared toilet and the whole landing was under three foot of water. Mam cried all the way home. Mind you, our Clayton did his share of blubbing when Donald got hold of him.

Come to think of it, the street what this Irma lives on looks strangely familiar. As I'm waddling up her front drive, looking left and right up the road, it all comes back to me: this is the one that the three of us was chased up by a gang of lads in Rangers shirts after we told them that all Scots were wankers.

Irma herself might not have taken too kindly to our observation, either. Despite a name what sounds like she's just stepped off the first plane from Vladivostock, turns out she talks like an Edinburgh wifie with an accent you couldn't cut with a chainsaw.

'Ah, Wattsy,' she says. 'How's the knuckles?'

'Not had a day's bother since I came to see you, Irma,' he says, talking like she's his long lost auntie or summat. 'This is my esteemed colleague, Mr Darren Tackle.'

'Hello, pet,' she goes. 'Come in and sit yersen down.'

Well, this Irma, she's about 107, all white hair and deffo no less than seven chins. I'd put her at twenty stone, minimum, with an arse so big she must need a police escort every time she visits Sainsbury's. And her gaff, my God. All these drapes and throws, and candles flickering everywhere. It's painted a sort of dark red and I don't suppose the curtains have been opened to access natural light for months. Actually, come to think of it, this is obviously where Mr Chairman's wife gets her decor ideas. That is when she's not having her interiors re-arranged by that bloke what runs a design consultancy on the High Street.

Anyhow, this Irma, she takes one look at me and says: 'Is it a fancy new sports car you drive? The big Jag? Or maybe the Ferrari?'

I says: 'You what?'

'Pet, I can spot it a mile off. They've been trooping in here once a week with the same complaint. Up from Man U., Liverpool, Blackburn. I've even had them down from Celtic. You young lads and your toys. I've told you all: get the garage to sort out the driving position before you set off. Anyhow, sit yourself down there, pet, and let Irma get her mind prepared.'

She makes me sit on a sort of pouffe at her feet while she dims the lights. Then she only gets a bottle of vodka out from this cupboard just down by her side and sinks back into her big old battered armchair (have to be big for her). She's obviously seen me eyeing the voddy up, but never even offers me a drop.

'Don't ask me why,' she says, 'but the healing powers only come when I've sunk a bottle of the good stuff.'

So we sit there in silence, me on a pouffe, Wattsy, Vic and Bob each in a corner and her, knocking back the Smirnoff like she's Boris Yeltsin's official taster.

When she's finally done, she asks me to take me shirt off and spin round on the pouffe. I'm a bit embarrassed, but sod it, we've come this far, why not descend into total humiliation; I'm expecting Bob to pull out his video camera any minute to send this sequence in to Terry Wogan on *Auntie's Sporting Bloomers*.

Then she puts her hands on me shoulders and stone me if I don't almost jump through the ceiling. Where the lovely Suzette has pre-warmed palms, this Irma's are like she's got a pair of ice mittens on. Then she starts slowly passing her hand over me back while humming a low note which will be very familiar to anyone what's fallen asleep in front of the telly.

'Er-rum,' she's going. 'Er-rum.'

Anyhow, obviously, I daren't catch Wattsy or Vic or Bob's eye because then I'll piss meself and the moment will be broken.

'Darren,' she finally says, after about twenty minutes of this chanting and touchy-feely stuff. 'Put your shirt on, pop the money in the plate by the door as you leave and tomorrow, all will be fine.'

That was it, was it, Wattsy? Drive all the way up to Blackpool so some twenty-stone bag lady can paw me all over with her leathery mitts? Trouble is, I can't give him what for, because he's gone all doe-eyed, kneeling at Irma's feet giving it plenty about how fantastic she is.

'Irma,' he's going, 'do you have any positive energy left for us?'

'Aye, pet,' she slurs. 'What can Irma help with?'

'Me ankle, Irma?' says Wattsy. 'And Robert here has got a tight hamstring, plus Victor's got a bit of a groin.'

So I have to stand there, bent double in pain, while the three of them is attended to. And after they've been done, and we've got out of her gaff, leaving – on Wattsy's insistence – a pony each in her in-tray, I can't hold it in any longer.

'Knob it, Wattsy, are you taking the piss or what?'

'Patience, my dear Dog, is a virtue,' he says. 'It takes a day or two for the healing hand of Irma to percolate through. In the meantime, gentlemen, we are in Blackpool, the party town of the north. So let's party.'

'Knob it, Wattsy,' I says. 'Let's get back. I can hardly stand up, never mind party.'

'Well my groin's feeling better already,' says Vic. 'In fact, let's put it to the test.'

You could tell, almost from when we start at this bar up by the north pier, what sort of night it's going to be. See, though the wind's whipping the waves up well up over the prom, and the rain's coming down horizontal, there's not a bird in the place dressed in more than three inches of material, in several cases not enough to cover the essentials. Chocker it is with lace tops and cleavage, acres of thigh and visible panty lines. Everyone's soon clocked who we are as we're stood at the bar, and sure enough the usual gap opens up round us like a forcefield.

Takes about ten minutes, but the first across the magic circle is a couple of slappers who tells us they're on a hen night up from Skelmersdale. Rough as a badger's arse they are, all drinking from little bottles of voddy and that they've brought in from the offie. You have to admire their sense of efficiency, mind: they was all drinking the stuff neat, through straws, the quicker to reach the point of total bladderage.

Within about two minutes, the inevitable's happened and the bird what's getting married is brought across to meet us. She's got L-plates sellotaped to her back, is off her box pissed, and is squawking on and on about how her Dean could've been a footballer and how, compared to him, we're all snotty, cocky and full of shite. Doesn't stop her, though, pulling her top up and insisting we've all got to sign her tits. Not easy for me, mind, putting me mark on a pair of whopping woolly-back bristols while bent double with the back pain. But, being a professional, I manage.

After that, we decide to move on, not least because a bunch of well dodgy lads has started chanting at us from the other end of the bar. Difficult to hear too clear over the sound of throbbing hard-core drum 'n' bass exactly what they was singing, but the words 'Darren', 'Tackle' and 'wanker' were deffo in there. We've been to four more bars, and I'm drinking to forget the pain, when Vic suggests we go to this place he's heard of called Dames Delite where they do a crackin' floor show, apparently.

As it happens, I can't remember too much about the place, except saying to Wattsy that the stripper at the end of the show has got a pair of pins on her which would not look out of place in our dressing-room. Not kidding: set of calves Roy Keane'd be proud of.

Certainly can't remember how I pulled one of the barmaids: sheer animal magnetism, I guess. Anyhow, she's a belter, big blonde hair, well stacked up top, dressed just in this basque affair, and like everyone else in this town, bleedin' Scottish. Still, before I know it, she's got me out the club and down this back alley and I've got me new Alexander McQueen pants round me ankles while she goes at it hammer and tongs, attending to me every need. On your bike Irma: this is what I call a laying-on of hands.

Not being selfish in any shape or form, after a couple of minutes activity down there (quite an expert at it she is, as it happens) I decide she deserves a bit of fun and all. So I pull her up off her knees, whip her round, push her face against the wall and start rummaging for an opening in her basque.

'You might get more than you bargained for down there, wee man,' she says. And to be honest, I take her point. It's worse than unlacing a pair of Ultima Tackles, her undergarments.

But then, when I'm in, I get the shock of me life. Let's just say, there was more in the undercarriage department than I was expecting. Not to put too fine a point on it, there's a bleedin' bloke in her briefs.

'Knob!' I screams.

'Well spotted,' it says. 'What was you expecting? You was in a trannie bar after all.'

So that explains the bleedin' stripper's legs. Well, I'm off out of there faster than a fast bastard. Round the corner I've gone, down the prom, legging it, buttoning me fly as I run. I do not stop hurtling until I reaches Wattsy's car which is parked up near Irma's place. Here I find Bob and Wattsy at it inside with four of the Skelmersdale hen night slappers, while Vic is standing guard outside eating a kebab. It's only after about five minutes trying to get me breath back and working out an alibi in me head about being chased down the prom by a dozen lads all chanting 'Darren Tackle is a wanker' that it occurs to me. Me back: it doesn't hurt any more.

Wednesday 11th

Two fried eggs and six Nurofen washed down with a bottle of banana milk, and I'm fit as a butcher's dog. I bounce into training, ready, able and gagging to put foot to leather once more. Wattsy, I have to say, is not looking his usual chipper self, with not so much bags as a full set of Louis Vuitton under his eyes. And Bob has got the makings of a Frank Bruno-scale shiner, caused, apparently, by a glancing blow from the knee of the Skem bride-to-be as they manoeuvred round the back seat of Wattsy's Merc.

We're all getting changed – in Wattsy and Bob's case very slow and deliberate – when the New Gaffer swans in. He's just about to start on one of his lectures about exploiting secondary possession when he stops and starts sniffing the air like a bloodhound.

'This changing-room stinks like brewery,' he goes. 'I do not want to know who, where, why or how. We are all adults here and I must trust you to find your own rules. But let me say this: drinking your English beer and being professional footballer, are, in my opinion, completely incompatible.'

He's looking at me, when he says that. Which is somewhat out of order: all night I was on that new Armenian bottled lager.

Monday 16th

Another bleedin' weekend off for internationals. Something's got to be done about this. Every time your decent, honest professional in the Premiership starts to get a bit of a rhythm going, we are rudely interrupted by the prima donnas flying off for pointless tin-pot internationals, played, in the case of several of the lads in our dressing-room, by pointless tin-pot international teams. Fair play, once again, then, to Alex Ferguson, who shows what he thinks of the whole club-versus-country scenario by giving his lads a quick kick in the achilles every time they get picked, which means they have to withdraw and stay back home where he can keep an eye on them.

You will have gathered, then, that Darren Tackle's international career is not progressing in any shape or form. It makes you wonder what they want, your Hoddles, your Browns and your whoever's-in-charge-of-Northern-Ireland-these-dayses. Are they interested in commitment or what? Because there's none more committed to the development of his career than yours truly. I was that convinced I'd get the call-up this week, I even had the telly repair geezer out to check the Teletext wasn't faulty. No, he tells me, there's nowt wrong with it. No Donald damage. He breaks it to me gentle that it was actually working fine and that my name really wasn't in any of the parties for this week.

'Stone me, Dazz, you must be gutted,' is how he puts it, all delicate-like. 'I mean, to be behind Andy Hinchcliffe in the queue for international recognition, that must hurt, mate. By the way, any chance of getting me Carmine's autograph. It's for me daughter, obviously.'

So, here I am, ready, spritely and up for it, back sorted thanks to Irma and I'm obliged to trot out with the left-overs, going through the motions with Old Demo, who, for some reason best known to the New Gaffer, remains in place to put us through ever more bollocks on the training ground. Today, for instance, he's got some pointless exercise he's heard the Brazilians use to brush up their skills.

'It involves heavy balls,' he says, a statement which leads to the inevitable bout of piss-taking. 'No, no, lads, I mean heavy balls like medicine balls. If you're not able to hoof it, the idea is, you have to caress it, make the ball your friend.'

Make the ball your friend? That would go against fifteen years of coaching I have experienced: 'clear it', that's the only message that's got through in my career. Anyhow, three minutes into the exercise and it's all gone pear-shaped. Vic's leathered the thing and Gary Ball's tried to get his nut on it and knocked himself spark out. Training session is abandoned as Wattsy, me, Vic and Bob take a limb each and carry the prostrate Bollocks back to the physio's room.

'Eh, Deems,' says Wattsy as we struggle back carrying the fat bastard who is clearly on a Snickers-only diet. 'I suppose this is what you call a heavy Ball.'

After we've got back in the changing-room, Demo pulls me over and says he wants a word. Private-like. Eh up. The call-up has come at last. I've no pride, me, about the international situation. I don't mind getting in there as a late replacement for Chris Sutton or whoever else has pulled out at the last minute in a fit of temper-temper. Just let me near them extra long 'uns.

'This isn't easy, Dazz,' he says. 'So I'll put it to you straight.'

'Don't worry about my feelings, Deems,' I says. 'You know me, Darren Tackle is such a squaddie, he'll turn out for anyone, anywhere, just for a game of football. So even if it's not England, I don't mind. Knob it, I'll play for Northern Ireland if the pay and conditions is right.'

'What you on about?' he says.

'International call-up, Deems. Who's it to be, then?'

'Yer what?'

'That's what you want a chat about innit?'

'No,' he says. 'Far from it. Fact is, the New Gaffer wants you to turn out for the reserves against Man U. on Wednesday.'

'The stiffs?' I says. 'You're having a laugh, incha?'

'No, Dazz. Straight up. You're in the reserves.'

This I cannot believe. After everything I've done for this club. They talk about us players not being loyal, but how about them showing some loyalty to us. Darren Tackle in the reserves: I tell him I won't do it.

'I won't do it,' I says.

'Just a moment ago, Darren, you just said you'd turn out for anyone,' he says.

'Hey,' I says, 'don't twist me words.'

So, on and on he goes about me adding a bit of experience, you know how the young lads look up to me and respect me and that. Besides, he says, I've got to prove myself to the New Gaffer out where it counts: on the park. So I says I suppose we'll all need to get match fit for Sunday, for the big one on Sky. I tell him I suppose Vic, Bob, Wattsy, all the non-international lads will be turning out with me and all.

'I get it, Deems,' I says. 'It's just routine, keep us all bubbling with some match practice, innit.'

'Well, no, Dazz, as it happens,' he says. 'Just you. The other lads will be taking some much-needed rest. And another thing: I wouldn't worry too much about Sunday if I was you.'

Tuesday 17th

After the indignity of training with the stiffs, on the way home I gets a call on the mobile from none other than Rodney.

'La-di-bleedin'-da, Rodders,' I says. 'Long time no hear. What's occurring, that assistant of yours lost his voice?'

'Listen, boy, joking apart,' he says. 'I need to have a – wossname – a word with you, private-like, face to face.'

'Too bleedin' right, Rodds,' I says. 'With some of the crap going on around me at the moment, you deffo needs to put in some hours.'

And I fills him in on the stiffs bollocks and the New Gaffer and Demo and that. I'm just about to get round to seeing what he could do about the Donald situation, when he interrupts me.

'Darren, Darren, Darren,' he says. 'You know full well it is golden rule numero uno of Rodney Gee Promotions Ltd (Putting the Showbiz into Soccer) that we on the management side do not get involved in the playing side at all. That is a complete and utter total exclusion zone as far as we is concerned.'

'Bollocks to that, Rods,' I says. 'You've always said you could get us a transfer whenever I fancied. Never stop going on about how George Graham and Terry Venables would always pick up the phone for Rodders. Summat's got to be done here, Rods, and you're the only geezer I know what can do it.'

'Tell you what I'll do, boy. Let's discuss this when we meet up. Can't say fairer than that, can I?'

'No probs with me, Rods,' I says. 'I'll pop round now. I'm just on me way to that bookie's near you as it is.'

'Not now, boy,' he says. 'I'm a bit tied up for the next few days, I'm about to land a couple of eggs what need a good boiling. I'll pop round to your house next Tuesday after training. You're not busy are you?'

'Busy with what exactly, Rods?' I says. 'When was the last time I got so much as a sniff of work for the afternoons?'

'Er, yes, boy,' he says. 'See you Tuesday. Speakcha.'

Wednesday 18th

They call the stiffs' games at our place 'Daewoo Family Football Fun Nights', a chance, apparently, to 'see your heroes in the flesh at a bargain price' (£15 adults, £9.95 concessions, with a 20 per cent saving on your half-time steak and kidney and reconstituted beef extract drink). In the dressing-room beforehand Old Demo – who gaffers the stiffs – says it's our chance to shine, because there'll be a big turn-out tonight, they'll all be wanting to catch Man U.

'What about us?' I says. 'Won't they be wanting to catch us?'

'Shouldn't think so, Dazz,' he comes back. 'Besides, they won't be seeing that much of you, because you're on the bench.'

As it happens, when we trots out, I reckon there's not more than 500 in there, scattered across the Alliance & Leicester main stand: a few kids in Man U. shirts, couple of Care in the Communities, all thinking they're going to be seeing the stars. Turns out we're up against ten pizza-faced fifteen-year-olds and Brian McClair.

And they give us the right runaround. Not that I can do much about it: I don't get off the bench all night. At one point I'm that bored just sat there watching teenage Mancs scoring at will, I pop back into the dressing-room for my mobile. Turns out there's four messages on it from Wattsy and that lot, all larging it down River Street for the night, taking the piss.

Afterwards McClair's in the players' lounge and I gets talking to him about this diary he writes for a football magazine. I says, who writes it for you? And he looks at me as if I'm daft and he says he does it himself.

'You what?' I says.

'I write it myself,' he says. 'Pen, paper, word processor, heard of them, Darren?'

I mean what's his problem? Surely at Old Trafford he's on enough to get someone in to do that sort of thing: why bark yourself when you can hire a dog, I say. No wonder he's always in the stiffs. No bleedin' initiative.

Friday 20th

Get in to training and find all the lads gathered round one of the posh papers. There's an article in there called 'The Continental Revolution', drooling on about the New Gaffer and his fancy foreign ways and how clever he is. Pathetic the way they're taken in: just because he wears glasses. Thing is, it comes complete, the article, with a picture of me, on the bench at the stiffs, talking on the mobile. The caption says: 'Wrong number: established British stars, like Darren Tackle, are finding themselves brushed aside by the new European broom sweeping through the Daihatsu Stadium.'

So that's the game is it? That's what everyone being given the chance to impress him means. What with this and the number 73 shirt, I'm beginning to think something's up; someone, somewhere's trying to tell me summat. But, hey, I'm a professional. I'll just knuckle down, graft and show this New Gaffer I'm indispensable. Wherever he's from, he's got to respect a touch of commitment.

And if it hasn't worked within the week, I'm off.

Saturday 21st

Go round me mam's to avoid bleedin' Donald and his pals and their building work and the only person what's round there is Hayley, our Lee's bird. She's still not popped and still cannot stop blubbin'. There's no sign of mam (out at Shoppalott), our Lee (out stacking shelves at same) or our Clayton (just out). Pity about Clayton. I just got the quote in for the Aston repair (a sum not unadjacent to twenty long 'uns) and I was hoping he might be able to do us a handy deal on a few parts to pull down me bottom line. Typical of the thoughtless sod to be out just when I needs him.

So I'm sitting on the sofa, next to this blubbin' mound of blubber, watching her from *Live and Kicking* droolin' on and on about David Beckham's legs, when the mobile rings. It's some wassock from Sky.

'How the hell did you get this number?' I says. 'You should bleedin' know by now all inquiries go through my agent.'

'Matter of fact, we got the number from Rodney Gee's office,' says the Sky wassock. 'He told us to call you direct. He says since you're *hors de combat* for tomorrow's big match here on Sky, you'd be available to join Richard Keys and Barry Venison in the half-time analysis box. The fee's £350.'

God knows what hors de bleedin' combat means, but £350 for sitting in the box instead of on the bench next to Old Demo and the New Gaffer seems like a sound deal to yours truly. In fact, I might just pop out now and pick up summat tidy down King Street, summat slick and fancy to show Barry Venison who's boss in the jacket stakes.

Sunday 22nd

Poor Venners. Probably thought he was going to stand out in that lime and crimson stripe with torquoise shirt and tie combination. But he'd not bargained for Darren Tackle, handily threaded out in head-to-toe Versace, complete with cravat, brocade frock coat and (cunningly not forgetting it's a three-quarter camera angle up in the Sky expert's box) jodhpurs in a subtle shade of custard. Only problem on the horizon is when Keys is so taken with me sartorial arrangements, he suggests the camera does a full-length pan and it only goes and reveals I'm wearing a pair of Nike trainers. Not, perhaps, the finishing touch I was looking for.

Especially when me mobile goes off in the middle of an ad break and it's Nigel the boot rep suggesting that, unless I wants a writ shoved so far up me arse I'd need an endoscope to read the fine print, I'd better get a pair of Ultima Tackles on pronto. A Sky minion is dispatched down to the dressing-room to bring up the aforementioned items. The things I bleedin' do for me sponsors.

Still, I think I managed to get me point across. Obviously you don't want to give too much away in these situations, but nobody could have been in doubt before the game started about what I thought were our chances, with all these fancy foreign tactics and the New Gaffer's new broom and some prima donna wuss like Carmine prancing and preening around up front. I said the way things is going at the Daihatsu, if we won today, I'd eat me trainers.

'Thank you, Darren Tackle, forthright as ever,' says Keys at full time. 'Oh, and here's a knife and fork. Because the fact of the matter is, that without their clairvoyant wing-back, the Greens have won for the first time in ten and won in style with a Carmine Perota hat-trick. And now news of the forthcoming Intel World Pool Challenge exclusively live on Sky Box Office 3.'

Sod it. And I suppose a slot on the National Lottery Show replacing Mystic Meg is out the question.

Monday 23rd

Oh yeah, it's all buzzin' in training all right. Bob arsing around in his new shoes, Gary 'Bollocks' Ball full of himself just because he got a slo-mo analysis from Andy Gray, Carmine's head's so big he'll have needed Pickfords to help him in to training. Knob: one win and all they think they're bleedin' Dennis Bergkamp.

Even Wattsy's at it, full of chat about my appearance on Sky.

'Sources tell me the Dog appeared on television as if ready to attend Gazza's wedding,' he says. 'And so leading edge, so post-ironic, so New Lad was it not to cap the entire canine ensemble with a pair of football boots.'

Course, as per bleedin' usual, everyone pisses themselves at everything Wattsy says. And I know for a fact by the look on his face that Bollocks didn't understand a word of it.

Me? I'm very much on the outside, looking in. It's made perfectly clear where I stand when Old Grandad, Mickey Scanlan, hands out a bunch of tickets for the dog racing tonight, to go and watch the greyhound what he owns the two back legs off-of, tear-arsing round the local track.

'What about me?' I says, when he's given out about a dozen.

'What about you?' he says.

'Don't I get a ticket?'

'First teamers only, Dazz,' he says. 'Bit of a reward for Sunday's performance. Remember it Dazz, Sunday? Remember how we won after some of the pundits give us no hope? Remember that, Dazz?'

Twat.

Tuesday 24th

Seems nothing can go wrong for certain people at the moment. Grandad's dog (the appropriately named Last Orders) come in at the back of a field of six. Bit of a coincidence, that, because it turns out Grandad's tipped everyone to back it to trail in last, and Wattsy alone picked up a long 'un. And how bleedin' handy a long 'un for yours truly would be at this precise moment in time. Because while the lads is filling their pants with readies last night, Darren Tackle is at home, trying to relax in front of *Goodnight Sweetheart* only to be interupted by Donald putting his step-ladder through the patio window.

'Never mind eh, lad,' is his considered response. 'Easy be able to get a new one as part of a job lot with the conservatory glass. Hey, and out the savings you'll get on that job, be a good lad and slip us a pony so I could get down the dogs with the boys for the night.'

Just as bleedin' well I've got this meet with Rodders after training. Leastwise, I thought I had. I'm just getting changed when I suddenly finds Demo in my face.

'Where you off to?' he says.

'That's for me to know and you to find out,' I says.

'Get your kit back on and get ready for another session,' he says.

'Eh?' I says. 'You don't get me on that malarkey. I've put me graft in today, now I'm off. I've got other fish to fry of an afternoon than just football you know.'

'Get your kit on,' he says. 'It's Tuesday. And every week that means a little extra afternoon session for the reserves.'

So that's it then. It's official. I'm a stiff. My mood is not helped by Wattsy, Vic, Bob, Darko and the rest waving a sarky bye-bye as they head off for a few afternoon sharpeners down at Mad Mick O'Shea's. Knob it. I tell you how bad it is being a stiff, by the time you gets out from extra afternoon training, there's not even any Care in the Communities hanging around the car-park looking for autographs.

I calls Rods on the mobile to tell him I'll be late for the appointment, and as per usual he's not there and I get that Tristram or whatever he's called.

'Oh, it's you,' is all he says.

'What's happened to Mr T, then?' I says.

'Oh, er, nothing,' he says. 'Rodney's not here.'

'Well tell him I've got to put back the meet for this after. Tell him to get round my place by about four thirty.'

'No,' he says. 'Can't do that. I'm sure Rods won't mind cancelling altogether. What he's got to say to you can wait.'

'Yeah, but I bleedin' mind cancelling. I've got a lot to discuss with him.'

'Yeah, well not today,' he says.

A bad day turns to total sewage when I gets home and discover Donald and two of his mates brickin' up the space where me patio windows used to be.

'What the knob is this?' I screams.

'Glad you like it, lad,' says Donald. 'Turns out your Clayton got his hands on a job lot of bricks from one of his contacts building the airport extension. Damned sight gentler on your pocket than a new set of patio doors, I can tell you, lad. You'll thank me when it's done.'

There's nothing for it but to head off to Mad Mick's and get in a skinful, see if life looks any better through a lager perspective. By the time I've got there, though, they've all gone, headed out to Dell's, according to Mad Mick.

'Aye, they all piled into Carmine's Ferrari and disappeared,' he says.

'Carmine's with them?' I says, thinking that just about sums it all up, that does: drinking with the bleedin' enemy.

'No, I never says that,' says Mick.

'Mick,' I says, 'you just said they all piled into his Ferrari.'

'I did indeed say they all piled into Carmine's Ferrari,' he says. 'But I never mentioned anything about Carmine being with them, did I?'

It's the little things, sometimes, what cheers you up.

Wednesday 25th

Bill, the fella from the *People*, rings me on the mobile on the way into training saying he wants to do an interview.

'Don't actually have to meet up, Dazz,' Bill says. 'I just want something along the lines of "End my Daihatsu Stadium misery", picture of you looking wellied off and then some bobbins about how you're desperate for a club to come in and rescue your career. Fifteen hundred suit you?'

'Cash?'

'Sorted. Who do you want to be linked with, anyhow?'

'Man U. and Arsenal, obviously.'

'Look, Dazz, we're into speculation here, not total fiction. How about Spurs and Everton?'

'But I'm not old enough for Spurs.'

'True, son, true. Make it Everton. Can tie it in with

claiming there's a renewed bid for the club by the Sultan of Brunei, as a present for one of his sons.'

'What you on about?' I says. Not a big one for papers, me. As a professional, I only get involved with the media and that if there's a drink in it for yours truly.

'Didn't you hear?' Bill goes. 'Apparently the Sultan lines up his three boys and asks each of them what they want for Christmas. First one says a car, so he buys him Rolls-Royce motors. Second one says a plane, so he buys him British Aerospace. And the little one says a Mickey Mouse outfit. So he buys him Everton Football Club.'

'Is that right?' I says. 'Wait till I tell Wattsy and the lads.'

'Dazz,' he says. 'It's a joke.'

Thursday 26th

I have to pop into the stadium on me way into training because me name's on the rota to sign the duvet covers in the HumungoStore. And I have to say, I'm a bit surprised by how tidy everything's looking. There's a whiff of paint about the place, there's a spruce-up going on; the old trout what normally sits on reception has been replaced by a Doris with a cleavage you could float the *Titanic* in, even the club secretary, a crusty sod what whinges every time you ask for an extra dozen comps for the Liverpool game, greets me with a cheery smile.

'Morning, Darren son,' he says. 'How's life in the reserves treating you?'

When I gets to the HumungoStore, I discover they've even cleared out all the old lines what they've been trying to flog off for months. Into the skip have gone the life-sized inflatable models of the old Boss, that was reduced to 99p. As have the collectors' jars containing the very water used to wash the team's shirts after our historic 3–2 home win over Man U. in 1992, retailing at £17.99 including limited-edition gold-effect plinth.

'What's going on?' I says to Eileen, the bird behind the counter, who, I can't help noticing, has popped on a little extra Estée Lauder this morning. She's been at the club years, Eileen. Developed a bit of a reputation for dropping her tangas for the juniors. Has a real taste for acne-covered seventeen-year-olds and pops down the kids' training ground at the first session of the year every year to make her choice. Some famous names have been brought to manhood by Eileen, I can tell you. And every year Wattsy opens a book on which apprentice will be the first to succumb to her opening her legs. It's what you might call our version of spread betting.

'Ooh, Darren Tackle,' she says as I walks in the store. 'You and me haven't had a one-on-one since that youth-team disco all them years ago.'

'Yeah, well, erm, enough of that,' I says. 'What's with the tidy-up?'

'Haven't you heard?' says Eileen. 'We're all going to be famous. Mr Chairman's got a load of telly people coming in to make a programme about little old us. You know, them flies on the wall.'

As it happens, after me marathon signing session (84 duvets, 78 team jigsaws, 105 Darren Tackle No. 73 shirts – apparently they've got a bit of stockpile at the moment), I bumps into Mr Chairman himself in the car-park.

'Ah, Tackle son,' he says. 'Glad I've run into you. I won't beat about the bush, you know me, tell it as it is, what's on me lung et cetera. Basically I've got a television crew coming in this morning, to film the rest of the season, show the club as it is, warts and all. No flim, no flam, no cover-up. So I want you well out of it. This film is meant to show as how we're a community club, decent, upright, fair-minded, exist simply for the fans. It's a fight back in the publicity war against them local busy-bodies poking their nose into my plans for an out-of-town super-stadium with integral hotel and shopping mall out by the new runway. I do not want them knob-heads from the fanzines round my place daubing paint on the drive the moment they find out what really goes on here. So I could do without tossers like you nausing up me PR. In the background at all times, right? Am I understood?'

Happy to be of service.

Friday 27th

On the way into training, I hear on the Chris Evans show that Ulrika's dumped Stan Collymore. Course I know precisely what the lads will be thinking, so as I walks into the dressing-room I give it plenty.

'Hey, Wattsy,' I goes. 'What's the betting on who's next to knob Ulrika? Mine's a century on Ian Dowie.'

And while I'm saying it, instead of everyone pissing themselves at the excellence of me banter, I notice Wattsy raising his eyebrows, nodding his head and looking like he's just had an electric current shoved up his nether regions.

'What's the matter with you, Wattsy?' I says. 'Got a twitch from too much wanking? What, doing it over an Ulrika calendar? Ooh, Ulrika-ka-ka-ka!'

And I'm bouncing around, doing the appropriate hand movements, and he's pulling these faces and shaking his head and behind him, there in the corner of the dressing-room, is Mr Chairman's fly-on-the-wall documentary crew filming our every move. Knob and sod it. I clean forgot all about them.

This could not have been more embarrassing. Thing is, I've only walked into the dressing-room with three brand-new pairs of Puma Kings slung over me shoulder. If Nigel, the boot rep, sees me carrying them instead of Ultima Tackles, on national telly, me bloody life will be a misery. Moment I realise what's going on, I've slung the offending boots under a bench, where they come to rest just next to Bob's new shoes. I think I got away with it. Least I didn't draw attention to meself.

MARCH

Monday 2nd

Transfer deadline day approaches, and still no word on a get-out. I can't understand it. Not a dickey bird from anyone. Not a single bid has been received for Darren Tackle. I tell you what and all, they'd be mad not to take me, these managers. There is no more committed pro than me. And right now I am totally committed to getting back in the first team. Anyone's first team. Oh aye, I'm getting frantic. If that was what was required to get me back in the big time, I'd get down on me knees and excavate Alex Ferguson's nether regions with me tongue. Yeah, I'd tack meself out as a drip-catching carpet round Kenny Dalglish's khazi. Hey, way I'm being treated at the moment, I'd have Jim Smith's love-child.

Mind you, the *People* done us no favours yesterday. 'RESCUE ME FROM DAIHATSU HELL-HOLE' was the headline above me interview. 'Desperate Tackle tells Evans, Gross and Dalglish: "Come and get me",' was the caption under a picture of me, wearing a prison uniform with these little arrows printed all over it while attached by ball and chain to the Burger King Memorial Gates outside the Alliance & Leicester stand. I mean, it made out like I had no dignity.

And as for the article itself, I'm sure I said it was off the record when I give that Bill them details about Carmine's major Grecian 2000 habit, Old Demo's fondness for rubber undergarments and Wattsy's recent brush with the law (in the gent's at Dell's, tried to buy two Gs off-of a geezer what turned out to be off-duty dibble; had to sort him off with a pair in the Allied Dunbar Executive Suite for the Arsenal game). And what was all this about the New Gaffer taking an unexpectedly close interest in the nine-year-olds at the School of Excellence? Seems to me the paper got a bleedin' lot for its fifteen hundred quid. I mean, Alan Shearer, he gets a couple of long 'uns a week for his diary in the *News of the World* and there's never more than absolutely sod-all in that.

So I knows what to expect when I sets off for training and, sure enough, the mobile rings just as I'm parking the Jeep (the Aston, since you're asking, is due to be returned from the body shop at the end of the week). It's Adele on the blower, saying the New Gaffer and Mr Chairman would like a word. But when I walks in to the New Gaffer's office, I sees we are not alone. As well as Mr Chairman and the New Gaffer, there's at least a dozen wassocks in goatee beards and rollneck jumpers, all leaping around with clip-boards and bits of wiring and what looks like hedgehogs superglued to the end of snooker cues – Mr Chairman's fly-on-the-wall documentary team.

'Act absolutely as if we're not here,' says the leading goateed wassock as I walks in. 'Just behave as if we are invisible. Pretend we do not exist. Put into your mind the concept that we occupy a parallel universe, merely observing, not participating.'

'You what?' I says.

'Ignore us,' says the cameraman.

'Oh, aye,' I says.

'Though having said that,' says the wassock, 'would you mind coming in once again and try to look a bit more nervous, worried, alarmed. Exude fear. Think terror. Be afraid. Be very afraid. And . . . action!'

So I walks in again, thinking about the last time I was in a car with Donald and the wassock gives it: 'Perhaps a little too afraid, luvvy, but it'll do for a first take.'

Mr Chairman, though, is clearly not acting normal. Very, very odd he is.

'We all make mistakes, son,' is what he says. 'But this is a family club and we look after our own. Close in around them. Enfold them in our love. I'm not going to fine you for this newspaper article, because I know how the press distorts things in this country. It saddens me to say this, but we live in a culture in which it is seen as clever to knock achievement. Besides, I don't want to upset the well-being of a crucial player at this crucial time of the season. So go out there, Tackle old son, and give them what for.'

I'm that surprised, I can't say a word, leaving Mr Chairman to say, 'That all right for you, gentlemen?' to the camera crew.

'I was hoping for a bit more, how can I put this, good television,' says the wassock. 'A row, a fight, tension, that kind of thing?'

'Well, you've picked the wrong club if you want that,' says Mr Chairman, with this totally unheard-of-before reasonable head on. 'One big happy family here. In't that right, Darren?'

'Oh, yeah, aye,' I says, just about getting me voice back from the shock.

'Pity, that,' says the wassock. 'Pity, that. Ah well, we'll head off to film training.'

'I'll show you the way,' I says.

'No, Darren, if you wouldn't mind staying back here until the crew has gone,' says Mr Chairman. 'Just got one or two tactical matters to discuss with you and the New Gaffer here.'

Tactical matters? Me? What's he on about?

It takes twenty minutes for the crew to leave the office.

I mean, talk about over-manned, there's more dead-beats in this lot than there is on Manchester City's pay-roll. And when they've gone I find out what exactly Mr Chairman means by tactical matters.

'You know me,' he says. 'I don't beat about the bush or prevaricate, say what I mean, think what I say, what's on me lung's on me tongue et cetera et cetera. And you, Darren Tackle, are a twat.'

And so it goes on; about how he'd never read such shite, about how the FA was going to bring a disrepute charge, about how the sponsors are threatening to withdraw support for the club because the article comes complete with a picture of me standing in front of their logo holding me nose and gagging.

'But Mr Chairman,' I says. 'You know what journalists are like. Like you says, I was mis-quoted.'

'Mis-quoted, my arse,' he says. 'That's why the paper invites us to ring an 0898 number and hear the full transcripts of the – and I quote – "Darren Tackle Daihatsu Misery Tapes". I've had enough of you. So I tell you what I'm going to do. I've told the New Gaffer here to put you back in the first team. Not because you're any good, because you're not, you're a twat. But because I want to off-load you, ship you out. And no one will pay a penny piece if you're stuck in the reserves. And right now I could use every penny piece I can get. One of my companies is suffering from a minor cash-flow problem. Though minor cash is probably all I'd bloody get for you. Now sod off out of here.'

Yesss! Result. Never mind the reason, I am made up. Any pro with any pride and self-esteem will tell you, there's only one place to be in a football club. And that's in the first team. Why? Because that's where the win bonuses are. And I'll need every bleedin' penny I can get after the fine Mr Chairman lands on me as I walks out the office.

Tuesday 3rd

Sod it. Just as I think things are getting back on track, there's a message on the mobile when I gets out of training. It's LeeAnne. Yeah, LeeAnne. The bird. Or should I say the ex-bird. Nine months I've not heard sod all from it, which suits me. Then, after all that blissful silence, here it is on the blower, like a scratched record. Says she's sick of it. Says she's going to sort me out for Krystalle's child maintenance at last. Says she's coming round Thursday after training and she's bringing that Rocky with her. Says she wants to see me. Oh aye. Not if I sees it first.

Wednesday 4th

Out the FA Cup, out the Coca-Cola, staring relegation in the face: now's the time you come together as a group of lads. One for all, and all for one. I tell you, the training ground is absolutely buzzing at the moment. We're all talking about Wattsy's plan for bringing Carmine down a peg or two once and for all.

He's been all over the papers, whingeing again (typical foreigner trick that, undermining the morale in the dressing-room by speaking out of turn to those whose job is just to do us down). Yeah, our 'wantaway South American' as he is known in the papers, has been up to his usual tricks slaggin' us off to all and sundry. I mean, your British pro, no matter how unhappy he is, keeps it all to himself. He just doesn't bleat. That is a no-no.

'Gentlemen,' Wattsy announces to a group of us. 'You all know the rules: no bleating. Today I am going to start issuing a few reminders of that rule. Beginning with our wantaway friend.'

Meanwhile Old Demo is setting up a line of cones for some crap new training idea he's picked up from watching the England cricket team prepare.

'Demo,' says Wattsy, waiting until the moment when he's put out the last cone, 'I don't know why you're bothering with that. We're doing five-a-sides this morning. And I'm picking sides.'

Course, Demo's got no choice. When Wattsy tells you, you do it. Now Carmine is, at this point, on the other side of the park, training on his own, so Demo is dispatched by Wattsy to bring him over for the game. And guess what? Carmine and Wattsy are on opposite sides.

Takes him ten minutes at least (Carmine's a slippery fish on the pitch) but eventually Wattsy lands a cracker, just above the eye. Kind of smack that means you can almost read the initials off-of his sovereign ring on Carmine's forehead. And the geezer goes down, squealing like a stuck pig.

'Ooooh, oooh,' he's going. 'Carmine, he has been, how you say, twatted good and proper.'

We're all standing round, nodding at Wattsy in recognition of the service he has provided to us all as Demo attempts to attend to the blubbin' ponce, when Old Grandad, Mickey Scanlan, suddenly pipes up.

'You prat, Watts,' he says. 'Sovving our best player, the one hope we've got of avoiding the drop. Have you got no bleedin' brain, you arsehole?'

There's a big silence from everyone (apart from Carmine, obviously, who's still moaning on the deck) as we all takes in the significance of this. But it's just the calm before the storm. Before you can say 'Keith Gillespie and the 3.30 at Market Rasen', Wattsy's lost his rag, is in there and the pair of them are at it, right in the middle of the training pitch.

It's over before it starts, and might have been forgotten as one of them things that happen between a bunch of lads. But who should be on hand, recording our every training-ground manoeuvre? That's right, Mr Chairman's gaggle of goatees, the fly-on-the-wall television documentary crew, all twelve of them. So they gets the lot.

'That will be good television, then,' I hears one of the goatees tell another as the dust settles on the barney.

This is the last thing Wattsy's image needs right now. You can hardly open the paper these days without reading yet another story about him. I mean the way the media and that constantly portray him, it's like he's some sort of nutter, a right hardcase, the biggest tough guy in British football. It's some bad-ass reputation he's got to carry. Now here's a camera recording him in scrap action. And the pisser is that Grandad dropped him with his first slap.

Thursday 5th

On the way into training, I checks the mobile and there's a message from Rodney saying he wants to have a chat. Probably about negotiating my appearance fee for the fly-on-the-wall. I'm just about to ring the geezer back, when the mobile goes off to say that the Aston's ready to be dropped off this afternoon.

'Will you be there to receive it, sir?' the geezer from the body shop says. 'Our insurance says there must be someone there to receive it.'

Too right I'll be there, I tells him. After what happened the last time when Donald got hold of the bleedin' thing, there is no way I'm letting anyone else anywhere near it.

'Drop it off about four,' I says. 'I'll deffo be back from training then.'

As it happens, I'm back earlier. After yesterday's little fracas, Old Demo decided it might be best if we left off the physical work for a while and did some classroom study this morning. So instead of a bit of useful five-a-sides, it was an hour in front of the whiteboard, with the New Gaffer telling us all about the need to alter our diet.

'We have to be more imaginative in our use of pasta,' he says, pointing to a load of squiggly shapes he's drawn on the whiteboard. 'Forget spaghetti. Think fusilli, twisty pasta. Or bucatini or tagliarini or this, linguini. Use any one you choose, but please with good sauce: tomato, garlic, herbs. Experiment, boys. Relax in the kitchen. Play your natural game. Use your flair, explore the possibilities. But always always always remember basics: use pasta.'

Afterwards I asks Wattsy – who, it has to be said, has the beginnings of one nonce of a shiner – if he fancies popping back to my gaff for a quick frame or two, stopping on the way for a doner at AbraKebabra.

'Have to decline the Dog's offer, I'm afraid,' he says. 'I'm off on my community service. Lecturing kids on the way to channel their aggression through football, not fighting.'

So I goes home on me own. Walks in through the door and nearly smack me jaw on the front step. What a bleedin' sight. There's not a speck of plaster left on me walls in the front room, it's just bare brickwork.

'A'right, lad,' says Donald, who's standing there applying the finishing touches to the bricked-up patio door. 'Thought your plasterwork was looking a little cracked, so while we were about it, me and the lads stripped it all off. We'll have your walls skimmed in no time, lad. By the way, any joy on that Carmine autograph?'

'Donald, where's everything gone, all me medals and the telly and that? Where's me PlayStation? I was in the middle of a game of bleedin' Virtua Pro Soccer,' I screams, taking in the scene of devastation.

'In the garage, lad,' he says.

'Did you save it?'

'What?'

'The game. The Virtua Pro Soccer?'

'No, lad. Just unplugged it. It's in the garage.'

'But Donald, I'd just got us to third in the Premiership with me as player-manager. And what the shag is this?' I says, pointing to the knobbin' great three-foot high pile of rubble in the middle of the carpet.

'Old plaster, lad.'

'Why's it in here?'

'See, I couldn't hire a skip because I'm stoney,' he says. 'Advance us a pony or two, there's a lad, and I'll get one in. Soon have this lot out.'

It's not even worth arguing with the geezer, so I cleans out me wallet, and decides there's only one place to take refuge: bed. I'm just on me way upstairs when the doorbell rings.

Oh knob. What with the Aston business and that, I'd clean forgot. And before I'd had a chance to warn Donald, he's opencd it up and she's there. Standing on the doorstep. LeeAnne, accompanied by a geezer the size of a small tower block: Rocky.

'I know he's here, so let us in,' she's gone, marching in and brushing Donald out the way.

'What the fuckenell is going on here?' she yells. 'My beautiful dream home looks like Fred West's bleedin' torture chamber.'

'A'right, LeeAnne,' I says.

'Don't a'right me, wankstain,' she says, silver-tongued as ever. 'Give us some bleedin' money or Rocky here'll have your kidneys out.'

'LeeAnne, I already gives you £150 a month, what more d'you want?'

'You haven't a clue, have you?' she says. 'I know what you're pulling down. I read the papers, you know. So I want some of it and I want it now.'

'LeeAnne,' I says. 'I'm borrasic. I've got sod-all. Don't believe what you read in the papers. Look at the state of this place, it's falling apart.'

'Shut it and give us your wallet,' she says.

'LeeAnne, you can have whatever's in it,' I says, chucking it over.

For once, Donald's played a blinder here. Destroyed me garden, turned me house into a khazi, then cleaned me out of readies. Good work, DIY fella.

'Fuck it, Dazz, I'm not here to mess about,' says LeeAnne, chucking the empty wallet in me face. 'Krystalle needs a new set of clothes for her auditions, I've not had anything decent for at least a month, and Rocky here's getting bleedin' impatient.'

Geezer looked it and all. Gorilla.

'All right,' I says. 'Just take summat.'

'Fuck it, Rocky,' says LeeAnne, running round the room, mad as a goose. 'Bastard's got fuck-all here worth having. I tell yer, Dazz, I'm fucking not remotely chuffed by this. And Rocky does a nice line in hamstrings, don't you Rocks?'

'Yeah,' grunts the gorilla, first thing it's said all afternoon.

'So Dazz, fuckin' cough up,' she says.

Just then there's a ring on the doorbell. I answers it and there's a geezer in overalls standing there.

'Mr Tackle?' he says. 'I've got your Aston on me wagon, where do you want it parked?'

Knob.

'Borrasic is you?' I hears the dulcet tones of LeeAnne as she emerges with her gorilla to stand there and look at ninety grand's worth of gleaming engineering about to be offloaded on to the drive. 'Rocky, get the keys off-of him. We'll have that.'

Treble knob.

Friday 6th

Still, one thing: Darren Tackle is in the first-team frame. On the coach, with the lads, back in the swing of it. On an overnight away for the first time in months.

We're staying in this Premier Travel Lodge on the ring-road outside Southampton. Normally I room with Wattsy, but he's suspended after that regrettable incident at Goodison involving the assistant referee's flag. So instead I've been put in with Old Grandad, Mickey Scanlan. The New Gaffer says it will be good for me to witness true professionalism at close quarters.

Grandad? Professional? He doesn't know what planet he's on, never mind what country he's in, the New Gaffer. See, any pro will tell you the proper routine for an overnight in a hotel is this: after the team talk, it's straight upstairs, order up summat from room service, hammer the mini-bar and have a furtive J. Arthur while watching the porn channel. Nothing beats a quick release of tension for putting you in the sleep frame of mind. And quality rest is an essential part of the professional's preparations these days.

But that's not for Grandad, oh no. First off, he's on the blower trilling to his kids for half an hour, so I can't order in a chicken club. Then, just as I'm settling down to *Butt-Happy Nurses on All Fours*, he's down in front of the telly giving it 400 sit-ups and obscuring my view of the plot. Worse, when I try to crack open a bottle of Molsen Ice from the mini-bar, I gets the full lecture on pre-match alcohol consumption. I tells him, a couple of bevvies never did Bryan Robson any harm, did it? Besides, it's medicinal, I needs them for sleep now I've lost the mood to bash the salami.

'Bryan Robson, eh?' he says. 'I knew Bryan Robson and let me tell you, Darren Tackle is no Bryan Robson.'

What is he on about? He even starts making tut-tutting noises when I gets stuck into the mini-bar's Toblerone.

'Darren, are you not aware,' he says, sounding like the bleedin' teachers at my school, 'that the club's nutritional advice is there for a purpose?'

But the final nause-up is when he puts a set of ear-plugs in, turns off the light, flicks off the telly and announces it's zed time.

'I'd like to point out it is nearly ten, Darren,' he says. 'New Gaffer's advice: every hour you're in bed before midnight is worth three after.'

Sick of this, I decides the only thing for it is to hit the bar in the lobby. As I'm walking past reception I spots the usual gang of anoraks. Three of them there are, with their sticker albums and their carrier bags full of coloured pens. I recognise them straight off as autograph completists, geezers whose idea of a good time is collecting every signature of every player of every team in the country, stalking hotels every weekend, waiting to wheeze their fish-paste breath over you while you sign every single one of their stupid books. It's a hazard of the game these days for us pros in the top flight.

Anyhow, I see they've seen me, but they're all hestitating. So I think, oh sod it, might as well get it over with.

'A'right, lads,' I say, popping on me he's-sound-in-real-life-that-Dazza head. 'Who shall I do first?'

'Er, thing is Dazz,' says one of them, looking all shifty. 'We don't need you.'

'You what?' I says.

'Yeah, well, see you're not in the new Merlin sticker collection. It's first-teamers only, see.'

First-teamers only? But I was in the shiny star-player slot in last year's album. I bought 237 packets of the bloody things down at Ali's, got 17 copies of me and stuck them all over the fridge. Now this year I'm not even in it. What the bloody hell's going on? And what's Rodders doing about it, that's what I want to know.

I'm that minged off by the whole affair that I slip down more than a couple of liquid sleeping pills at the bar. Couple of hours later, I gets back to the room, gets me kit off and falls into bed spark out.

Course, about three in the morning, nature calls and I'm in significant need of a visit to the facilities. You know, there is an urgent requirement to siphon the Tackle python, not to mention drop a couple of kids off at the pool. So I opens the bathroom door, walks in and for a second I'm confused, trying to get my bearings and work out what's what, and more to the point, where's where. I've only just clocked the geography, when I hears the door behind me swing to and shut, click. And yes. I've only opened the wrong door. I'm standing out there in the corridor, starkers, locked out me room.

So I knocks on the door and there's no bleedin' answer. I knocks again as loud as I can without drawing attention to meself. But of course, Old Grandad's got his bleedin' ear plugs in. Well I can't knock on anyone else's door, can I? Imagine the slaughter if Darren Tackle knocked on Vic's or Bob's or, worse, the two sixteen-year-old YTS lads-brought-along-for-the-experience's door at three in the morning while stark naked.

But I'm not stupid. I've remembered there's an emergency phone by the lifts. So, I bells down to reception and explains the situation. I needs help, and pronto.

'I'm sorry, sir, but I'm on my own down here,' says the Doris on duty. 'There's nothing I can do to help.'

'But I'm in the corridor, bollocks on full display and bursting for a piss,' I says. 'If that doesn't constitute an emergency, I don't know what does.'

'I'm sorry, sir,' she says. 'I'll see if I can find someone to help. But it may be some time.'

Some time? It's months. I'm just stood there, naked, looking up and down the corridor, expecting another guest to come along at any minute, cupping me embarrassment. And no one comes to rescue us. After about ten minutes, I'm that desperate, I have to relieve meself in a potted plant. While I'm doing it, I spots the shoe-polishing machine and thinks to meself, what would it be like to stick me naked foot under the revolving brush.

Well, I'm that bored with waiting, I try it, using the suede-only facility, obviously. Turns out, it's quite tidy, a gentle, rotating motion, pleasantly buffing the skin. Handy feeling as it happens.

So, checking no one's coming, I gets down on me knees and – well you know what I'm saying – try it out elsewhere. Nice. I'm just getting to grips with it, when there's a tap on me shoulder, I nearly jumps out of me skin and there is an unhappy engagement between shoe cleaning machine and naked body part. You could have heard the scream in Bournemouth.

'Aaaaagh,' I goes.

'Oh, sorry, Dazz. Didn't realise it was you,' says this voice behind me. I'm hopping around in agony, but through me tears I can just make out who it is. It's only one of the bleedin' autograph completists. 'What the bloody hell are you doing here?' I says, jumping from foot to foot, bell-end throbbing.

'Thing is, Dazz,' he wheezes. 'I was standing at reception hoping to get the last couple of signatures to complete me Greens section, and the woman behind the counter asks me to come up here and let a guest in what's locked out.

She's given me the master key, see. You haven't seen anyone locked out, have yer?'

'It's me, you prat,' I says, still – it has to be said – somewhat in agony. 'What you bleedin' waitin' for? Let me in.'

'You, Dazz?' geezer goes.

'Well why else do you think I'm out here?' I says.

'I wouldn't like to say,' he goes.

'Just let me in, will yer?'

'I'm thinking, Dazz, mebbes we could do a little trade-off. I'll let you in if you could do us a favour.'

'Look, if all you want's me autograph after all, no problem, I forgive you,' I says. 'Just let us in.'

'Thing is, Dazz,' says the geezer. 'It's not yours I want. If I let you in, you couldn't get us Carmine's could you?'

Sunday 8th

I'm not looking for excuses, obviously. Darren Tackle is not one to hide behind the cop-out. Or shy away from facing the consequences of his actions. But is it any wonder the *People* only give us a two for the performance I put in against Southampton yesterday after all that?

Tuesday 10th

He's gone. Finally, totally, completely. And this time for good. Carmine has packed his bags at last and fled the Daihatsu Stadium for some Portuguese second-division outfit and enough pesos – or whatever they have over there – to re-plaster my front room. In his hurry to get the hell out of England, our wantaway South American left behind the following:

1. A wardrobe full of Patrick Cox loafers, seventeen pairs of which were still in boxes.

2. Mr Snipz, that wussy hairdresser in the Old Market, facing bankruptcy.

3. Some pitiful Care in the Community blubbing in the *Sun* about how he'd just had Carmine's face tattooed on his buttocks. And worse, it cost him a week's dole and the bloke at the tattoo parlour won't give him a refund. And you can't say you can really blame the tattooist geezer: how's he going to re-sell a picture what's printed on someone else's bum cheeks?

4. Some slapper quoted in the *News of the World* saying he'd promised to marry her.

5. Another one in the *Sunday Mirror* claiming not only had he promised to marry her, but that he's said he had seven brothers back in Paraguay for all her mates and all.

6. Three other paternity suits, including one from a sixty-year-old hill farmer from Yorkshire.

7. A dry-cleaning bill from some West Ham fan who claimed he spat at her when we last went to Upton Park. 'These fancy dan footballers, they think they're a law unto themselves,' the alleged gob victim was quoted as saying in the *Mirror*. 'It was a completely unprovoked attack. All I did was call him a greedy lazy wop bastard ponce and he spat at me.'

8. A warehouse full of unsold 'You are my Carmine, my only Carmine' T-shirts.

9. Seven complaints to the police after his goal celebration at Blackburn. 'There were young children

in the crowd,' one fan told the *Star*. 'And frankly there could be no doubt in anyone's mind what he intended to do with that corner flag.'

10. An exclusive with every national newspaper football correspondent about how crap English football is, how the training stinks and how English players are just interested in getting bladdered, the horses and doing lines of Gianluca with Page Three girls in nightclub toilets.

11. The bailiff acting on behalf of Oddbins demanding payment for fifteen cases of champagne and a bottle of strawberry dacquiri; a £7,500 tab at Coral's; and Marco, the bloke what can usually do you a handy G down River Street on a Saturday night, threatening to break his knee-caps should he ever show his face in town again. 'I'm a businessman, not a charity,' Marco told Wattsy when he rang for the first team's usual weekend R & R supply. 'And that Carmine geezer, he took some liberties with credit.'

12. £800 worth of damage at the Orange Aubergine, that new restaurant down by the canal, after an altercation with two fans, an autograph book, a set of Sabatier knives and an ironing board.

13. Three columns in posh papers lamenting the loss of the greatest talent the club has ever seen. One article was headlined: 'THE JEWEL IN THE CESS-PIT'. I mean, you have to wonder sometimes what them spekky students what write the clever papers are on about. Basically all Carmine did was go down like he's been hit by small-arms fire the minute he strayed into the oppo box. Okay so he was handy with a football, could pass the thing like no one I'd ever come across. Plus there was that goal he scored at White Hart Lane when he beat every single Spurs player twice and popped it between the keeper's

legs with a back heel. But what the middle-class droolers should be asking is where was he when the thermometer takes a nosedive and we're drawn in the Cup against a bunch of non-league shin-saboteurs on some rain-lashed bog covered with so much sand you don't need a long stud so much as a bucket and spade strapped to each foot? Buggering off to warmer climes pronto, that's where.

14. One Ferrari, still wrapped round a lamp-post outside Dell's, where Wattsy and that lot left it after borrowing it for the night.

15. An unpaid mobile phone bill of £2,676, of which more than £2,500 was spent on ringing up the Green Line Club Call to hear himself being interviewed by Gabby Yorath.

16. Our dressing-room cock-a-hoop, now that he's gone and he's taken his constant undermining of morale and that with him. At the regular team meeting, after training down at Mad Mick O'Shea's pub, we all chipped in with ideas of how to mark his departure with a special celebration next time we score a goal. Wattsy's idea was for us all to get down on hands and knees and snort the eighteen-yard line; Vic suggested a mime where we all pretend to take out girlie make-up mirrors and do our hair; but my favourite was Bob, who said that we should all turn and face Paraguay, you know like Muslims and that lot face Mecca when they're praying, and then give it a synchronised V-sign. Lovely-jubbly.

Just one drawback: without Carmine, us scoring a goal's about as likely as seeing Jim Smith on the box endorsing his own range of hair-care products.

Wednesday 11th

Message from Rodders on the mobile. He wants to talk, urgent, he says.

'Bell me, boy,' he says. 'We need to parlay. Speakcha.'

You bet we need to parlay. Expect he wants to apologise for his pitiful performance in sorting me out some off-field action to balance the fine situation. I mean, we're supposed to be in the middle of a football bandwagon here. Football is supposed to be fashionable right now. According to the wassock with the goatee masterminding the chairman's fly-on-the-wall documentary, we should all forget flat caps and whippets, football is suddenly Gaultier suits and ciabatta. So how come Darren Tackle's not getting any of it? Wattsy told us he'd heard on the grapevine that them Richard and Judy off-of morning telly got a free kitchen when they opened up their lovely home to *Hello!* magazine the other week. Straight up. Apparently, magazine pops a new cooker, freezer, the works in there just to persuade them to let some hyena of a journalist loose on their soft furnishings. Would it be asking too much of Rodders to sort me a similar deal involving a new set of patio doors and some glazing work in the conservatory? I think not.

Course, when I ring back he's not there. And that Tristram or whatever he's called, he isn't there neither. All I gets is an ansafone message saying: 'This is Rodney Gee Football Promotions Ltd: Putting the Showbiz into Soccer. I'm afraid all our executives are too busy making money for our clients to take your call right now. But if you'd like to leave a message we'll get back to you as soon as we've completed yet another successful deal.'

The message I left was short and to the point.

Thursday 12th

Whatever the reason Carmine done his runner only he can tell us. What we as lads must do is knuckle down and get on with keeping this club's Premiership status alive. And what we have to do is make sure that our concentration and preparation are not disturbed by all this speculation about the geezer in the media and that. We just have to be professional and accept it as part and parcel of the typical media over-reaction which we inside football must learn to expect these days.

That said, there is no denying that some of the scenes on that preview tape of Mr Chairman's fly-on-the-wall documentary which was leaked to the papers yesterday might be misconstrued as somewhat embarrassing. And yes, I have to accept that there is some truth in the rumours being spread around about the incident with Carmine when we was staying at the Ramada outside Leeds a couple of weeks ago. But to suggest that was the final straw in his departure is just speculation, taken well out of context.

So allow me, if you will, to fill in the details so sadly lacking in the media and that. Basically what happened was this: Bob, right, our resident enthusiast for all things turd-shaped, collects a bunch of Richards in a plastic carrier bag, sneaks into Carmine's room at the Ramada while the geezer's doing his standard 300 lengths in the pool, and leaves them strategically lying around the place. Now that must be seen for what it was: part of the laugh you have as a group of lads. It was certainly not, as the papers have ludicrously suggested, just one stage in an orchestrated campaign to force Carmine out of the club. I mean, there was nothing orchestrated about it. We all just had a go now and then. Only for the laughs, obviously.

Unlike all these media types who feel qualified to pass judgment without any first-hand knowledge of the situation whatsoever, I was actually there. So I'm in a position to tell you what actually happened. Well, for legal reasons, I have to admit I wasn't actually there, I was in the hotel bar at the time. But I have talked to those actually involved first-hand, so I actually have got a pretty good overall sort of impression.

For me, it was all down to a sense of humour failure on the part of the hotel manager. When Bob rang reception and complained about the smell emanating from Carmine's room, the manager should have spotted he was just having a giggle. Particularly the bit about the Paraguayan's pathological inability to use a flush toilet. He certainly should not have thrown Carmine out the hotel, despite, when he inspected the room, finding the first five chapters of the Gideon Bible in an unhappy condition, the complimentary fruit bowl with a couple of less than fragrant additions and the button on the remote control which accessed the porn channel permanently depressed thanks to some unusual adhesive.

What the camera doesn't show – typically – is that, as Carmine was being frog-marched out the place escorted by the local dibble, several of the lads were ready to jump to his defence and tell the management it was all a practical joke. And they would have succeeded if Vic, Bob and Wattsy hadn't threatened to punch their lights out for sneaking.

Now that that is cleared up (the situation, I mean; I think the club paid to have Carmine's room sorted straight away) let's hope the media and that will let the personnel of this football club get back to the important matter in hand. That is – though I can assure you the word is not being uttered in this dressing-room – the threat of relegation. And more particularly the pressing need to sort out a transfer over the summer to make sure we'll all still be playing in the Premiership next season.

Friday 13th

Another message on the mobile from Rodders ('Bell me, boy, I'm suffering withdrawal symptoms from not talking. Speakcha'). Again he's not there when I rings back. I must ask Wattsy what Eric Hall's number is.

Saturday 14th

I'm on the touchline again, down in the dug-out, the non-playing sub trussed up in the merchandise department's new designer bench range. Not the kind of clobber you would wish to be seen dead in. Unfortunately, it is becoming a worrying habit is this: Tackle surplus to requirements. And because I'm excused games, I thus miss out on the battle of the century in this afternoon's six-pointer relegation dog-fight.

My God, it was like Vietnam out there. It was boiling up all game, but the final spark was when Wattsy – back in the side for the first time since his three-match ban – has a bit of a tangle with their centre back on the touchline right by the dug-outs and decides to extricate himself by drop-kicking the geezer in the head. You could hear the thud echoing right round the Alliance & Leicester stand. Bit of tooth landed in the fourth official's lap.

Course, soon as it's happened, everyone's up off the benches and joining in for a bit of handbags. It's got well out of order, some of the crowd's in there, stewards, dibble, the lot. When the dust has settled, the final toll is three red cards for us, two for them, three stretcher cases, five arrests and Old Demo needing medical attention for a blood-pressure-related condition. Still, at the end of the day, we gets a point out of it, so it can't be all bad.

Afterwards, I was expecting the New Gaffer to read the riot act. That's the usual way with Bosses: beforehand they tell you to go out there and die for the cause, then after, when you've taken them at their word and fetched up with a card or two, they start chucking the fines around. But that's not the New Gaffer's way. All he said was, we was all adults and we had to decide for ourselves whether we had behaved inappropriately and let the club down. That's an easy one then. No disrespect to the fella, but is he a wuss or what?

Still, he has the last laugh. He's just finished speaking when he turns to me and utters the words every pro dreads.

'Darren,' he says, 'as you were not playing today and were therefore one of few not to be sent off, will you please do press?'

Not that. Not the bleedin' press. An hour with Motty, the knobheads from the nationals, the shouty radio guys, not to mention the sad losers from the local papers, when I could be in the bar putting the incidents of this afternoon behind me with the assistance of a bottle or two of Molsen. Jesus Knob, the things you have to do for football.

As it happens, Motty's first up, recording the interview down outside the dressing-rooms in front of the sponsors' logo board. Important place, the sponsors' logo board. Get your head in exactly the right spot so the right logo is bang smack in the middle of the viewer's field of vision and there's an extra long 'un in your pay packet. It takes me ten minutes to sort it exactly right – blocking out the ones what don't pay with me shoulder, twisting me neck to display the good 'uns – during which time Motty and his cameraman are getting well agitated. But perfectionism is what marks out the true pro.

'Darren Tackle, thanks for joining me,' says Motty, when we eventually gets started. 'I must ask you first of all about the Michael Watts incident. What was your view of it?'

Well, my view of it was the best in the house, Wattsy attempting on-field root canal work on their lad using the most rudimentary of dental techniques. You could almost hear him saying: 'Sorry, mate, haven't brought my micro-fine drilling equipment with me today, so I'll have to attend to that dodgy molar of yours using only my studs.'

Course, I've been on media training courses, so what I actually says was this: 'Well, John, I can't really comment on the incident because, as I say, I didn't actually see it.'

'But Dazz,' says Motty, 'it happened three feet away from you.'

'I was actually watching the game at the time,' I says. 'I mean, all I know is that Wattsy is a true professional and I can assure you there certainly would not have been any malice in the incident. From what I understand, Wattsy merely became entangled with their lad and, while he was trying to extricate himself, the lad's face unfortunately came into contact with his boot. Nothing more than that.'

'Well,' comes back Motty, 'perhaps you'd like to have a look at the monitor here at an action replay, which I think appears to show that – quite possibly – you were the first one on to the field when the scuffling broke out.'

'To be honest with you, John,' I says, 'I really wouldn't like to comment on any attempt at trial by television.'

And so it goes on, through Radio 5, the in-breds in the press room, right down to the local radio guys. All of them asking the same bollocks: 'How did you view the Wattsy incident, Dazz?'

Answer: 'From the dug-out.'

'Are you going to miss Carmine in the run-in?'

Answer: 'Not if we contract a good sniper.'

'How do you see the relegation issue sorting itself?'

Answer: 'With three clubs going down and the rest staying up.'

Sadly, these answers didn't come to me until about three hours later, but I think I just about got away with it. What I could've done without is the clever gets from the Sunday posh papers sitting in the back row of the press conference room, wetting themselves at everything I says.

'So let me get this straight, Dazz,' says one of them. 'You think it's better at this stage in the season to have points on the board over games in hand, but games in hand are there to be won and points on the board aren't much good if you haven't got them. Is that right?'

But the whole thing was put into perspective when I did the local paper lads. There was only two of them there, instead of the usual three. That Slimey Simon from the local *Times*, who's been at every Green game I can remember, wasn't there. Pity really, you could always rely on him for a Green-tinted view. It would have made a change from all these hyenas trying to do the club down going on about Wattsy and Carmine and that to have Slimey S. telling us how, whatever happens, the Greens are and always will be better than the Blues. I made a joke to the other two about him being fined for missing his first game for forty years, but they didn't laugh.

'Haven't you heard, Dazz?' says one of them.

'What?' I says.

'He passed away this morning.'

'No.'

'Straight up, Dazz.'

Poor geezer. He'd been around for ever doing the local scene. He used to cover me when I played for Flixton St-Germain in the kids' league. He done the write-up for me debut for the Greens. Me mam had a scrap book consisting entirely of his reports about me what our Clayton nicked and sold to some saddo collector for

95p. And now he's dead. Not Clayton, obviously. I mean the journalist fella.

'Puts a few sendings-off into perspective, eh Dazz?' one of the lads says.

'Aye, too right it does,' I says. 'What did he, you know . . . What was it what, that, you know . . .'

'The Big C,' one of them says.

'What?' I says. 'You mean he couldn't swim?'

Sunday 22nd

PFA dinner.

Monday 23rd

All right, since you ask, the PFA dinner went like this. I have to say I was not in the best mood when I arrives. I mean, I don't want to sound bitter, but what is going on? Because as per bloody usual, there is not a dickey bird of a mention of a certain no-nonsense, tough-tackling, over-lapping wing-back in the short-list for Footballer of the Year. Your Bergkamps, your Seamans, your Beckhams, oh yeah, they're all in there. Even our late and not particularly lamented whingeing foreigner's had a couple of nods from sad sods what don't know better. But yours truly? Nothing. Darren Tackle is once more ignored by the footballing establishment.

What more are you supposed to do to get noticed in this game? I mean, it's not as if I've kept a low profile. It's been some season I've had. I've been invited twice (no less) on to *The Footballers' Football Show* on Sky; I've had three mentions in Greavsie's Saturday column in the

Sun; plus it was me what worked out that goal celebration with formation All Saints impressions as featured on *They Think It's All Over*. Oh, and Alan Hansen devoted the whole entire chunk of his analysis on *Match of the Day* to my contribution to our 5–0 defeat at Old Trafford (I reckon if you strip away some of that telly punter jargon – you know them words like woeful and abject – Hansen was basically agreeing with me that most of it was down to bad luck).

And, as if to prove the point, there I am again taking a central role in the *News at Ten* report about a fracas outside the PFA dinner with them feminist pickets, upset that no women is ever invited to the bash. I mean, what are they on about, all them lesbos? Of course women is allowed in to the PFA dinner. What do they think all them waitresses are? Wattsy gets a slap regular as clockwork every year for getting a bit fresh with the serving dollies.

To be fair, the *News at Ten* incident happened after the Player of the Year had been announced. But it just goes to underline what a big rick my peers in the PFA made by not recognising the all-round contribution to the game made this season by Darren Tackle.

My less than chuffed mood was not enhanced by being made to sit on the club's second table, along with Mr Chairman, Old Demo and the New Gaffer, who spent the entire evening telling me about the life-enhancing properties of the great god mineral water. All the rest of the first-team lads – Wattsy, Vic, Bob, Darko, Bubbles, Hermann, the lot of them – were at a table together, chucking bread rolls at Richard Keys, booing every mention of Man U., ringing up Ian Wright's mobile and asking him who he'd most like to have a One-2-One with. In short, having the kind of tip-top time you'd expect from a bunch of pros. Meanwhile the talk at our table is about how fresh fruit naturally rids the body of excess toxins.

I get so sick of it, that, mumbling something about a

pressing need for the khazi, I make it to the bar, hoping for a fill-up before joining the lads. I'm just standing there, waiting for the barman to fix us a pint or three, when this voice pipes up next to me.

'Mmm, you're smaller than you look on television.'

I turn round and am confronted by this six foot streak of wuss, wearing an earring and a complicated wing-collar arrangement on his dinner shirt.

'Don't recognise me with my clothes on, do you Mr T,' it says. 'I'm Tristram. Or should I say Fi-Fi the Flounder.'

Bleedinell. Then it occurs to me: if he's here then Rodders must be here and all. And boy do I need his services right now.

'Where's Rods?' I says.

'Very much the chatty Mr T as per usual,' says this Tristram, or whatever he's called. 'Since you ask he's up the other end of the bar.'

'Where?' I says.

'There,' says this Tristram. 'Talking to Les Ferdinand.'

The bar's packed (Gordon Taylor's speech has just started, see) and it takes me a while to fight me way over to him, what with all the chats and that I have on the way, but there at the end of the bar, sure enough, is Rodders and Sir Les.

'Rods, thank God you're here,' I says, after letting on to Les.

'Not now, not now,' Rods says. 'I'm busy.'

'No, no, Dazz, Mr Gee, don't worry about me,' says Les, looking a touch relieved to be interrupted, turning on his heels and disappearing away from the bar, it has to be said, at the sort of speed Spurs fans haven't seen for a bit.

'What's your game, boy?' says Rodders. 'I was in there. About to land the biggest fish of them all and now you've scared him off.'

'Yeah, well my need is pressing,' I says. 'I'm sitting at the table with Mr Chairman and the New Gaffer and I should be at the table with the lads. There's been a right cock-up, I've been put on the management table and there's not even the lovely Suzette to talk to because she was banned from coming because she's a woman.'

'What you on about, boy?' he says. 'I'm not quite following the drift you wish to pursue.'

'What I'm saying is I can't have a decent bevvy, Rodders.'

'And?'

'Well, go and sort it for us, eh?'

'Who do you think I am, boy?'

'Me agent.'

'And what do you think agents are for, boy?'

'They're for getting the dosh in, innit?'

'Since you seem unsure what your particular agent does for you, let me fill you in,' he says. 'The way you appear to see it is that agents are for ringing up the sponsors to apologise after their client has turned up two hours late at a personal appearance and then proceeded to interfere with one of the hostesses. Agents are for schmoozing the boot company which paid £50,000 for their client's services when said client has just been photographed by the papers with half a dozen boots of another manufacturer slung over his shoulder. Agents are for turning up at disciplinary hearings to support their client when no one else will. Is your antenna drifting on to the particular wave-length I am pursuing, boy?'

'Yeah,' I says, not getting his drift at all. 'So will you sort the seating arrangements out then or what?'

'No,' he says.

'But you're my agent.'

'Not any more I'm not.'

'What you talking about, Rods?'

'I've been trying to tell you for weeks, boy,' he says.

'It's over. I've earned precisely sod-all off-of you this last six months. If Rodney Gee Football Promotions Ltd relied on you, the whole geseft would've gone muhullah months ago. All you have brought me is grief, grief and more grief. Oh, and then some more grief. I've got bigger eggs to boil, boy. Now you're on your own. Rodney Gee is moving into the big time and he does not need wasters like you no more. Now, if you'll excuse me I've just spotted Michael Owen over there.'

Sod him.

I wonder if that Tristram or whatever he's called fancies breaking out on his own?

Tuesday 24th

When I wakes up yesterday afternoon (training is always a no-no the day after the PFA) and made me way downstairs for an overdose of Nurofen and six gallons of orange juice, I could not believe the bleedin' mess Donald has made of me kitchen. Everything tipped all over the place, drawers out, cutlery scattered all over the floor, the microwave smashed, me Come On You Mighty Greens picture calendar ripped into shreds. What the knob has that twat been up to now?

I go off screaming round the gaff looking for the geezer and find him cowering in the conservatory, where the scene is no happier. All the snooker cues are lying around broken into firewood, what remaining windows there are have been smashed by the snooker balls which is all now lying out on the lawn. Meanwhile the snooker triangle is embedded in the middle of the team photo taken in the Stadio del Alpe the season we got into the UEFA Cup (lost 6–0 to Torino, as it happens, but I still reckon to this day the ref had took an envelope).

'Donald, what the knob—' I says.

'Don't you remember, lad?' he says.

'Remember what?'

'What happened when you got back last night.'

'Bleedinell, Donald, I'd been to the PFA dinner. Of course I don't remember what happened last night.'

'Well, I'll tell you lad. I were woken up by the sound of smashing glass. I come running down thinking it's souvenir hunters after your underpants again. And I find you, smashing the place up screaming as how you're going to kill them all.'

'Kill who?'

'Rodney, the New Gaffer, Mr Chairman, the PFA for not letting the lovely Suzette in to the dinner. You weren't being choosy, lad.'

Knob. It's beginning to come back. I look around the snooker room. And out into the garden. Knob: it really is beginning to come back.

'So what's that taxi doing out front?' I says, sort of half thinking I know the answer and didn't want to hear any more.

'You got a cab home,' says Donald.

'Aye. So why's it in the ornamental pond?'

'You want to know?'

'Depends.'

'Then you don't want to know.'

'No, tell us Donald.'

'Okay. You and Wattsy gets a minicab from where the team coach dropped you after the dinner, right?' he says. Yeah, it's beginning to come back. 'You persuade the driver to wait outside while you have a few in Dell's before chucking out time, then you gets back in and tell him to go to that all-night curry house – Ringstingahzi or whatever it's called – down by the university. Course, he's made up, fare's up to £275 by now, geezer'll go anywhere. When you gets to Ring's you says to the geezer, is there any chance of him popping in to see if the coast's clear? You know, check if there's any punters in there what might mither. Fella's only too happy to help, jumps out the cab and legs it into the curry house. And while he's in there, the old alcohol homing instinct kicks in, you have to get home and immediately. Pronto. Now. So you climbs into the front seat, and drives home. And you ends up parking in the pond.'

I looks down. I'm still in me black tie – handy Dolce & Gabbana collarless Nehru jacket as it happens – but it's covered in this green slime. Pond weed.

'How the hell do you know all this, Donald?'

'Wattsy told me. He kipped here, left an hour ago. By the way, he says if the wife rings, to tell her he deffo wasn't round here. Seems she'd told him she'd leave him if he ever mixed with you again. So he'd prefer her to think he was out with a bird than hanging with the likes of you.'

Knob it. If all this is true, that Rodney has got one hell of a lot to answer for.

APRIL

Wednesday 1st

You can always rely on the lads to cheer you up when you're feeling a bit low. And at the moment I make Doncaster Rovers look buoyant. But that's the great thing about being a professional footballer (apart from the money, and the birds and the fame and that): the banter in the dressing-room won't let anyone stay low long. And of course, today is the day when, across the land, Premiership or Unibond, Nationwide or Dr Marten's, the dressing-room banter is riper than a Gazza fart.

It makes me laugh sometimes when you hear what the media and that think we footballers do for a giggle. I mean, no one in the modern game goes in for all that cutting the ends off each other's socks, chucking the gaffer into the team bath fully clothed or putting Deep Heat in your mucker's under-snags any more. The game as a whole has moved on from that: things is much more sophisticated and modern in the banter department. Well, it is at the Daihatsu for certain.

Here we know how to have a laugh. The best gag of today, for instance, centred on one of the Bosnians. A couple of months ago, the geezer was out for a month after he came up in real bad boils and stuff. His skin bubbled away that mingin' everyone was joking that he was trying to join Man U. by developing a pizza-face like all them kids in their stiffs. But after the club doctor's conducted a ton of tests on him, turns out the fella's only contracted scurvy. Eventually they prize out of his interpreter that he's addicted to Pot Noodles. Geezer's not eaten anything else since he's been over here. Up to a dozen a day. We are talking one humungo instant snack habit. When the New Gaffer hears this, he's got him in and put him on an intense diet: all complex carbohydrates and polyunsaturated enzymes or summat. To help wean him off his addiction, Pot Noodles are subsequently banned from the premises, which is somewhat of a shame as I am more than partial to the Spicy Curry flavour meself. Bosnian bloke, meanwhile, gets better, gets back in the team, but lets it be known through his people that he'd die for a Pot Noodle after training.

Well, it being April Fool's Day, Bob's thought he'd oblige. Course, it being a Bob Pot Noodle, there was a marginal adjustment to the flavouring. Bob bought a Sausage 'N' Tomato one, carefully slipped off the silver foil cover, tipped out half the contents, replaced them with some runny Richard what he had just produced, then popped back the silver foil and, with the aid of a Pritt stick, re-sealed the job. Or should I say the big job. After training, he offers it to the geezer, whose little face is a picture (albeit a touch pock-marked). Fella adds boiling water and then proceeds to wolf it down as if it's the last bit of nourishment this side of Sarajevo, not even noticing Bob's special ingredient. And of course nobody says a word, just lets him get on with eating shit.

See what I mean? Clever.

Thursday 2nd

Wattsy's little April Fool's gag, on the other hand, was neither funny, clever nor grown up. After training yesterday, he bounds up to me and says: 'The Dog is back.'

'You what?' I says.

'Let out of quarantine,' he says. 'Every dog has his day and the Dog's is tonight.'

'Eh?'

'I just overheard Demo and the New Gaffer talking through the team for tonight,' he says. 'The Dog is back in. Central midfield role. Skipper and all, in the absence of Grandad.'

Course, I'm made up. And I bounce over to where I can see the New Gaffer and Demo standing having a chat what I assume is about yours truly and the role he will be undertaking tonight. So I'm hovering there like a right keenie and the New Gaffer turns round and asks if he can help.

'I understand I'm in the team, Gaffs,' I says. 'Central midfield. Skipper in place of Grandad. Spect you was just about to tell us.'

It has to be said, judging by the look on his face, this appears to be news to the New Gaffer.

'You in central midfield?' he says.

'Aye,' I says.

'No, Darren, there must be mistake,' he says. 'We must win tonight's match. So you are not in the team.'

And with that he turns back to Demo and continues some conversation about introducing a new regime of warm-down stretches. And I turns round and sees Wattsy, Vic, Bob and the others all standing there doing universally recognised synchronised movements with their hands which denote you believe someone to be a wanker.

See what I mean? Not clever.

Friday 3rd

Commitment. That's what this club needs right now. Professionals absolutely dedicated to the cause in hand, namely saving our Premiership win bonuses. This is no time for faint hearts or those who do not want to stay aboard the bus for the long journey that is the Daihatsu Stadium project. I've convinced meself of this on the way into training, and after the whole squad've done the few warm-ups and stretch-downs that constitute a session at this time of the season, I've decided to have it out with the New Gaffer.

I've cornered him and told him that what he needs at this time is me. Badly. I said that this is the time of the season when you need lads what you would want beside you in the trenches. That is, if the Premiership was a re-run of the First World War. Which, in many ways, like when you go to Selhurst Park, it is. You want good lads, honest lads what you can rely on, stand shoulder-to-shoulder with. And, though I obviously wasn't trying to threaten him or owt, I adds that if Darren Tackle's not in the frame for a game at this of all times, then Darren Tackle's clearly got no future here. Over the summer, it'll be best if he packed his bags and looked at life beyond the Daihatsu. Harsh words, I know, specially at this time when everyone's pulling together and that. But they had to be spoken.

And you know what he said to me, the New Gaffer?

'Darren, on your way out, would you fetch that pile of bibs over to where first team's about to have game of five-a-side? Thank you very much indeed.'

Saturday 4th

It's taken a while for it all to sink in – the shirt number 73 business, the dropping, the never getting back in – but it's all now fallen into place. Never mind what that teacher said at school about Darren Tackle, he's not thick, he can read the signs. The New Gaffer just doesn't fancy me: he wants me out. At least now I've come to recognise where I stand.

Actually at this moment in time, I'm not standing at all. I'm sitting on the sofa at mam's house, where I've taken refuge for a week or so while Donald and his mates do a final bit of patch-up work on my gaff. He's promised it'll be ready by the time the season ends when I'll be looking to off-load it before moving into some massive pile in Cheshire or Southport or wherever, depending on who signs me. Not forgetting, there's some handy properties in Hertfordshire I've been told, should Arsène Wenger show his hand, which obviously he's keeping close to his chest just now. All in all, best be prepared, property-wise.

Mam's, though, is not the most restful place for an athlete. That Hayley, Lee's bird, what seemed to have been expecting for about three year has finally produced a baby what bawls night and day. This sets Hayley off a-blubbin' and mam, in an apparent attempt to drown out all the sobbing, has gone on a hoover frenzy. Plus the phone is ringing off the hook with geezers trying to get hold of our Lee or our Clayton, neither of which has stepped foot inside mam's gaff the entire time I've been there. So there's me, trying to relax with me Virtua Pro Soccer what I rescued from me garage, surrounded by more bleedin' noise than there's been in the Daihatsu all season. The only thing what's quiet is my mobile, out of which I have not had the merest hint of a peep for over a month now.

Now, course I know the rules. We all know the rules

and anyone what breaks them has only themselves to blame if they gets found out. It's quite clear: no player is allowed in a premises what sells alcoholic drink up to forty-eight hours before a match. That includes subs and non-playing members of the squad what might be called upon to turn out in the event of injury. Hey, we're grown-ups, we understand rules. And tomorrow is a big tense one on Sky against the Arse. Clear heads is what is needed all round.

But I think even the New Gaffer would appreciate that, for this particular athlete, a quiet pint down at the Ferret & Pie Stall would be better for his mental preparation than staying at his mam's place listening to a re-run of the Gulf War. Unfortunately, when I've got to the Ferry I've forgotten it's Saturday night. The gaff is packed, heaving. All I can do is swallow hard, keep me head down and hope there's no bastard Blue in the place what'll shop us to the New Gaffer.

But, keeping me head down isn't that easy an option, specially as the place is swollen with blart, tott bulging from every corner. Everywhere I looks there's birds in micro-shorts and top knots and tits so inflated Richard Branson could use them to fly the Atlantic and there's a DJ giving it some well happenin' anthems and there's a Grolsch promotion on and there's a lot of lights and action and everyone's havin' a crack and everyone's lettin' on to me and buyin' us drinks because I'm a footballer and after midnight there's a two-for-the-price-of-one run on the Smirnoff and I spots Marco in the gents and he gives us something to keep us going and I'm up on the dance floor largin' it big-style and the next thing I knows is it's 3.30 in the morning and I'm down the alleyway round the back of the pub and there's a bird dressed in bugger-all snorting a line of Gianluca off-of the bonnet of the Jeep while I attempt to unclip her spangly Wonderbra and when I gets to me mam's house I finds that Hayley still up and blubbin' on the sofa about how our Lee never comes home and when he does he never pays her any attention and how he's left her holding the baby and the next thing I knows we're on the living-room carpet and I've got me mitts on her blobby bastard baby milk tits and me mam comes in and finds us givin' it plenty and Hayley starts blubbin' again as she pulls up her shreddies and mam gives it both barrels askin' me how I could do it to our Lee and this Hayley, she's blubbin' even louder and she starts slaggin' me and sayin' it's my bleedin' fault and how I'm that big-headed and that and how I think just 'cos I'm a footballer I can have anyone I wants and I says fuck the lot of youse and goes back to my gaff and ends up kippin' in the Jeep because Donald's changed the locks on the front door without tellin' us.

Some might say not the ideal preparation for a professional athlete the night before a crucial relegation scrap. But after the week I've just had, there's one thing to be said for it: at least it took me mind off-of the football.

Sunday 5th

Another defeat. Hey, don't blame Darren Tackle. He watched it from the stands, not even deemed a sufficient part of the set-up to warrant a place on the bench. There's some minds want concentrating round here, because if this situation isn't sorted pronto, that clause in me contract with the boot company about not getting any bonuses if we get relegated is in serious danger of being invoked. And that kind of nause is the last thing I need in my life right now.

Monday 6th

Old Demo pulls me to one side after training. Fourteen calls there were to the club about me being seen at the Ferry on Saturday night. Some tossers really have no life, do they?

'We get calls every week about lads breaking the embargo, Dazz,' he says. 'And I accept most is bollocks.'

'Yeah and these is bollocks, Deems, I was at mam's.'

'Fourteen, Dazz,' he says. 'You can't ignore fourteen calls.'

'Yeah, from tossers.'

'One was from the Chairman's wife,' he says.

'Doesn't wear a spangly Wonderbra does she?'

Knob.

'All right, I admit I was there, Deems,' I says. 'But I only popped out for a mineral water. Me mam had run out, see.'

'A mineral water?' he says. 'That's why one bloke said he saw you on the dance floor at 2 a.m. attempting a Northern Soul back flip. It must have been needing a mineral water piss that took you into the gents at 2.30 when another geezer says he saw you emerging from the cubicle in the company of two blokes, all three of you sniffing. And that mineral water must have gone straight to your head, because a third caller says he was standing at the bar with you at 3 a.m. where he bet you a tenner that you couldn't hang three beer mugs off your knob, and you paid up after managing only a half-pint pot.'

'That's all bollocks, Deems,' I says. 'It was deffo a pint pot.'

Tuesday 7th

During training, I starts getting serious jip down the base of me spine, shooting pains when I try to run, real nasty, real uncomfortable and I have to pack it in. This I cannot believe. Just as I needs me full fitness head on to prove everyone wrong, I've got a recurrence of the old lower-back problem. But when I gets to the physio's room, hoping for ten minutes or so under the fingers of the lovely Suzette, there's a long line already forming for her soothing services. Mickey Scanlan, Old Grandad, he's at the head of it, ready to climb aboard the table, and he tells me in his usual charming way to wait my turn.

'Piss off to the back of the queue, Tackle,' he says. 'Priority cases only. And right now you is so far down the priority list it'll be the middle of next season before you're looked at.'

As it happens, an hour and a half it is, watching Grandad and the rest being pummelled and pampered before I gets anywhere near the lovely Suzette. And when I gets there, it all goes pear-shaped. Big-time.

I tell her me problem, shooting pains up me spine, not able to run comfortably, and she pops me on the table and probes around me lower back for about ten minutes, but can find no tender patches.

'It's a bit lower down, to be honest,' I says. And I explains it's a kind of stinging sensation in me nether regions.

Suzette makes knowing noises, then asks me to do summat I've been waiting to do for her all season: drop me trolleys.

'On to the table, Darren, please, on all fours,' she says. Now, I have to admit, this wasn't quite what I was expecting. Maybe they do things different in France. But she's manoeuvred me round, on me hands and knees, naked bum pointing skywards, head down. And it occurs to me this is a position what wouldn't be the first you'd adopt if you were wanting to cop off with a fancy foreign bird.

'As I thought,' she says, examining, not to put too fine a point on it, me arsehole with an implement what looks like a tyre pressure gauge. 'Piles.'

There's not a lot else to do, as I'm up there, dignity in tatters, with apparently a bunch of chalfonts dangling in the breeze like grapes, except turn round, look over me shoulder, wink seductively at her and say: 'Fancy a curry tonight, love?'

Wednesday 8th

I take it easy at training, you know, a bit ginger, a bit careful. And afterwards, as I'm making me way to the dressing-room dreaming of the bucket of ice I'll be dipping me arse into, the wassock with the goatee from Mr Chairman's fly-on-the-wall documentary team corners us.

'Darren, luvvy, would you mind just doing us a quick one-on-one? Ten minutes, no more.'

'You'll have to speak to me agent about this,' I says.

'Sorry?' says the wassock.

'You'll have to . . . No, on second thoughts don't worry. Where do you want us?'

Their first mistake is to try and record the interview out in the open, just by the changing-rooms. This is both thoughtless, and, if I might say so, very dangerous. For nearly half an hour, as the goateed wassock attempts to put his questions, I am vulnerable to all sorts of attacks of the kind you get the moment you bring a television camera out in the open at a football training ground. First off it's Vic, chucking bits of rolled-up newspaper at us everytime I open me gob and making us laugh. Then it's Wattsy approaching with a hosepipe. And when Bob weighs into view, coming from the direction of the changing-room gents and carrying a bucket, with a purposeful look on his face, I suggest it might be best for all concerned if we head off indoors, double-quick style.

Once we're there, and the lighting geezer's happy with his lighting and the sound geezer's happy with his sound and some bird with a clipboard has got me to sign some bollocks piece of paper that she says I needs to sign if I wants to get me appearance fee (get us a pen pronto), the wassock tells me he wants to hear a different voice in his film.

'I want to hear the voice of frustration, Darren,' he says. 'I want to balance the triumphalism of the first-teamers. I want to know what it is like to be on the outside, when you have once been on the inside. I want to know the disappointment, the bafflement, the world-weary sense of rejection that informs the very soul, the very heartbeat of those not sitting at high table on black-tie dining night.'

'You what?' I says.

'He wants to know what it's like to be in the stiffs,' says the cameraman.

So I tell him.

Thursday 9th

Transfer deadline day passes without any action on the yours-truly front. I can only assume that this is a consequence of the Bosman ruling. Everyone's holding fire, hoping to pick us up in the summer when I'm out of contract and they won't need to pay a fee. Either that or no one wants us.

No, no. It's Bosman.

Friday 10th

'Easter time is very vital / That's when we decide the title.'

That's my favourite line of poetry, that is. It was written by John Toshack, who's an old geezer what played for Liverpool back in the dim mists of time. And though he must be close to ga-ga now, the geezer they knew as Tosh wrote anything but. He certainly knew a thing or two about football. Because while you lot are down the DIY superstore stocking up on lime-free compost and patio paving slabs or whatever it is you normal people do of an Easter weekend, we professionals are facing up to the toughest time of the year. Sweat will be sweated, blood will be bled, tears will be teared, or whatever. Make no mistake about it, this is when it's all decided. Will it be Man U. or the Arse for the title? Who'll nab the European places? And, more importantly for my particular near-term future, who'll be going down with the Palace?

Such thoughts have been preoccupying all of us this week. And Wattsy, knowing how everyone's mind will be on the vital Easter weekend programme, has thoughtfully opened a book. Me, I've put a century on us going down. Look upon it as a bit of insurance.

Saturday 11th

It couldn't have come at a worse time: the club is deep in injury crisis, we are losing top men left, right and centre. It literally looks like the Battle of the Somme in our dressing-room right now. Well, not exactly like it, obviously, there's no mud or guns or rats chewing at open wounds as the shells fall. But it's grim enough in there.

Vic's done his hamstring stretching up to the top shelf at his local newsagents for something to relax his mind with at home, Darko's gone down with a knee problem from the dodgy driving position on his new tractor-style lawnmower he bought to cut the grass in his fifteen-acre garden and the Pot Noodle Bosnian has been hospitalised with some stomach complaint. Malingerer.

Add in the usual hand of suspensions what plague you at this time of year – Wattsy's out for another three for that unfortunate misunderstanding at Coventry, when his attempt to give the referee his whistle back was misconstrued as an assault simply because the fella had to undergo an emergency six-hour operation to remove the blockage from his colon – and that £100 of mine looks distinctly like a Bank of England investment.

And the chances of me playing meself have taken a serious tumble with this pile business, what's giving me major jip. If push came to shove I could play – I'm probably 98 per cent fit. Maybe 99. But at the moment, realistically, for the kind of rough and tumble of the Easter weekend programme, you need to be up there in the 110s.

At first I'm gutted when I realise that when I'm asked to play, I'll have to rule meself out. But then it occurs to me it's another shrewd bit of insurance by yours truly to make himself unavailable right now. Any professional will tell you, if your club is staring relegation in the face, this is the time of year to hide. When you're looking for a new employer after you've gone down with the Palace, you don't want to be tarred with the brush of failure by actually turning out during the death throes.

As a professional, obviously, I'd have to turn out. And I'd give it the full percentage for the entire ninety minutes. But it would be a mistake. Fortunately embarrassment all round is averted when no one asks me to play.

Monday 13th

Along with no booze, funny food, endless stretching exercises and treating us all like adults, the New Gaffer's got another completely alien idea: charity week. Once a month we're meant to set up a series of little rules among ourselves what if anyone breaks they have to pay a fine. At the end of the week, all the fines are totted up and sent to a charity. Supposed to create team spirit, bond us as a group of lads. Comical or what? How is giving our money away supposed to make us a better set of lads? How is that meant to be better for team morale than going out on one of Wattsy's gentlemen's competitive pulling evenings? Foreigners, see. No clue.

Don't get me wrong, Darren Tackle is all for charity, and always makes himself available for first nights, sportsmen's dinners, the Charity Shield (well, never actually got there, but I would if we did), any event, in short, where there's a few snappers from the papers and an envelope at the end of the night to compensate us for time wasted.

Anyhow, at the team meeting, the New Gaffer asks if anyone has got any ideas for fines for charity week this week. So far we've had a load of mingin' stuff – about wearing the right tie, or having your boots clean, or arriving at training on time, all suggested by Mickey Scanlan, who is rapidly degenerating into New Gaffer's chief anal passage cleansing operative. Needless to say, I went down for a pony or two.

So this time, I'm in there the moment the subject is raised, making sure the odds is stacked well away from the direction of yours truly.

'What about a fine for every time someone's mobile rings?' I says, knowing full well mine hasn't tinkled since the bleedin' Ice Age.

'Excellent, Darren,' says the New Gaffer, looking somewhat taken aback. 'Maybe I underestimate you.

And how much do you suggest we are fined for mobile ringing?'

'Hey, New Gaffer, we all want to raise as much for charity as we can, don't we? How about a long 'un a time?'

'A long 'un? Fuck off, Dazz,' says Vic, voicing what I was hoping might be the general feeling. 'You can shove that bollocks.'

'No, no, no, that is excellent idea,' says the New Gaffer. 'Thank you Darren, that is settled. And what exactly is "long 'un"?'

I tell you, if looks could kill, at that moment, the entire squad would've been up on a murder charge.

Friday 17th

End of the charity week, four days of relentless do-goodery and not one bastard has been copped with a ringing mobile in training. Thus raising not one solitary sov for charity. As for the New Gaffer's other purpose in bringing in the idea, morale is at rock bottom as everyone is giga-hacked off at being detached from their umbilical to the outside world for up to two hours a day.

Mind you, it has created a certain unity among the other lads: every single one of them wants to deck me. Wattsy was screaming this morning about how turning off the mobile's naused up his chance of picking up the bad-boy's role in a forthcoming McDonald's advert featuring Alan Shearer; Darko's mithering on because he didn't collect the dry-cleaning what his bird had left a message on his mobile for him to do; even Mickey Scanlan's whingeing because he missed a call from his poxy son to tell him he'd just been picked for his poncey prep-school hockey team. Worse, Bob's not saying a word. Which makes me fear some hideous toilet revenge. Sooner this sodding week ends the better.

No training today, instead we're all in the meeting-room listening to the New Gaffer who gives us a two-hour lecture about how if we want to get out of this relegation hole, we must re-prioritise our approach to second-phase possession, or summat. I'm looking round to see who's nodded off, and all I'm getting is bad vibes; every time I catch someone's eye the scowl I gets in response is poisonous.

Then suddenly, just as the New Gaffer's got to some nonce about channels of integration and support of the player on the gain line, a mobile rings. It's like an electric shock's just run through the room. Every bastard freezes and looks round, checking out who's about to go down for a long 'un. The New Gaffer stops rabbiting. It rings on. No one's answering it. It rings on. No one wants to cop for the fine.

'Come on, who is phone?' says the New Gaffer. 'Answer it, pay fine, we get on.'

But no one answers. It carries on ringing. Whoever's not answering is playing it well cool. Though the New Gaffer doesn't seem too happy.

'Come on, hurry,' he says. 'We have relegation to worry about, answer phone.'

Everyone's looking at each other, but no one answers. Then Wattsy looks at me, points and shouts.

'It's the Dog's dog! It's coming from him!'

'Nah,' I says. 'Can't be.'

'It is. It's the Dog's bastard phone. Yessss!'

And it is. I haven't turned the twat off because no one's rung us for so long I just never bothered. I get it out, and try to answer it all subtle-like, but everyone's jeering and laughing and that.

'Hello?' I whispers, trying not to draw any more attention to meself than I already have.

'Ah, lad,' says this voice at the other end. 'It's Donald. Bit of a problem at the gaff. While we was just connecting up the new conservatory, 'fraid your, er, back wall just collapsed. Nothing we can't sort, lad. But it might put the re-build schedule back a week or two.'

Monday 20th

'April is the cruellest month.' Some other geezer, not John Toshack, wrote that. And I tell you what, for a poet, fella knew his football. When you're down there in the bottom three, April is bleedin' horrible.

Things is getting well tense round here. The telly has been going on and on and on about what'll happen to Mr Chairman's cash-flow if we go down, radio phone-ins are filled with yonners ringing in to whine about how they didn't pay good money for season tickets to watch us go down, you can't open a paper that isn't at it, comparing us to the great Green sides of the past. 'DAIHATSU HALL OF SHAME' was the headline in the *Mirror* over a picture of this year's squad. I wouldn't mind, but I was singled out for special mention. Bit rich or what? I've only played three times since Christmas.

And Mr Chairman's fly-on-the-wall documentary crew isn't helping matters: the goateed wassock's been poking his nose into every nook, cranny and conversation, asking his stupid questions what no one understands. 'Spiritually, as it were, how is the prospect of demotion viewed within the framework of the competitive ethic?' – that was one.

Fortunately for him and his stupid programme, his cameraman's around to translate: 'Is you lot crapping your trolleys about going down or what?'

Course, being professionals we ignore the media and

that and just get on with motivating ourselves as individuals. We all have our own routines. Some focus on past performances, others remind theirselves how good they really are, some use meditation techniques to clear the mind completely for the task in hand. My own particular method involves blocking out everything, media, the lot, and concentrating on one thing: just making sure I play well enough so them bastards in the *People* give us a decent mark out of ten. Nothing ridiculous or over-ambitious, a solid seven would be nice. All right, a six.

Tuesday 21st

After training, I gets pulled over by Old Demo.

'Dazz, it's looking bad,' he says. 'Seventeen pros out with injuries or suspensions. Add in a bunch of the youth team going down with an allergic reaction to the course of anti-acne tablets they've been taking, and we've literally got fifteen players left in the club who can play on Saturday. We've tried the FA, but they won't let us bring in anyone on loan. We would cancel, but look what happened to Middlesbrough couple of years ago when they tried that game. Dazz, we're that desperate you'll have to play.'

'But, Deems,' I says. 'Me piles.'

'We've thought of that,' he says. 'New Gaffer's dietician has come up with a roughage-only diet that you'll be on for the rest of the week. Should have cleared up enough by Monday.'

Knob. Or rather, arseholes.

Thursday 23rd

Bob comes up to us after training.

'Dog,' he says. 'Can I have a quiet word?'

'Sure,' I says.

He leads us into the changing-room bogs and locks the door behind us, all conspiratorial, checking over his shoulder all the time to see if anyone's watching.

'I hear the Dog's on a roughage-only diet,' he whispers.

'Bleedin' right,' I says. 'It's like chewing wood-shavings. My mouth feels like I've spent the night on the floor at the Ferret & Pie Stall with me gob open.'

'Yeah, right, listen,' he says. 'On all that bran and that, you should be getting some nice solid samples. Useful for a little blag I'm working on for Mr Chairman's fly-on-the-wall documentary team. Take these home and fill 'em, would ya? There's a good Dog.'

And he hands me a bunch of plastic bags.

Friday 24th

Back at mam's. I've no other option. Donald's put scaffolding round the house, but forgot when he was doing it about the front door, putting a pole right down the middle of it so you can't get in nor out. I ring him on the mobile on the way over to mam's and ask him what the bloody hell he's playing at and he says he don't understand what I'm on about. Why didn't I walk in through the big hole what used to be the back wall like everyone else, he says. Also he's put back the schedule for completing all the work.

'We're talking late July at the earliest, lad,' he says.

'After all, lot of the lads'll be wanting to watch the World Cup. By the way, can you get your mitts on any tickets? Me and the boys quite fancy a little trip to see Carmine step out for Paraguay.'

Sunday 26th

Wake up rather pleased with meself. Despite that Hayley and her brat bawlin' and blubbin', despite mam constantly cleaning round me feet, despite the phone ringing itself stupid with geezers looking for our Clayton and our Lee what are never in (including some bloke asking if I knew whether our Clayton still had that set of Jeep alloys what he was peddling around a couple of month back), despite all that, I stayed in all evening and even got in one of Mickey Scanlan's early nights.

So, you can imagine, I'm feeling pretty smug when I gets down to breakfast (All Bran with bran-flake topping, as it happens) only to be confronted by mam with a face on her about three yards long.

'Darren, what the bleedinell are these?' she says, plonking a bunch of plastic bags with long, windy Richards in them into my bowl, splatting milk and All Bran all over me sweatshirt. 'I found them stuck behind the cistern when I was cleaning the toilet and Hayley swears they're nowt to do with her or the baby.'

'Thanks for reminding me, mam,' I says, grabbing them up and legging it out the house. 'I needs them for training and I'd forgot.'

We've got an extra session with tomorrow night's game in mind and just before we starts, I give the bags to Bob who seems well chuffed.

'What you going to do with them?' I says.

'Hush-hush, Dog,' he says, tapping the side of his nose.

'But I tell you it's a big 'un. I'm going to give them goatees summat they won't forget in a hurry.'

When training starts, I'm feeling on top of me game, as it happens. Piles have stopped giving us jip, all in all I'm cruisin', tip-top and ready. I've just done a fancy one-two with Darko, stuck the ball through the Gary 'Bollocks' Ball's legs and is just about to show who is the top Dog round here by slotting home the decider in a frantic game of next-goal-wins five-a-sides, when I'm brought down with a clatter. I never even seen him coming, but it was Wattsy what done it, clipped me on the ankles and I've gone over and I'm rolling around in agony. The lovely Suzette is called up from the physio's room and as I'm laying there looking up at a huddle of concerned faces (though, come to think of it, Wattsy, Vic and Bob didn't look that perturbed) she delivers the words no one in the entire Daihatsu set-up wants to hear at this particular moment in time.

'Twisted ankle, Gaffer. He's definitely out for tomorrow.'

A silence falls as everyone takes in the significance of this news. It's finally broken by Demo, who says, 'Never mind, Gaffer, he was only going to be sub anyhow, I'm sure we can busk it through with one of the YTS kids.'

Monday 27th

Said YTS kid comes off the bench at the end of this crucial relegation six-pointer and scores twice to give us our first away win of the season. What a result.

I tell you, I've travelled with the lads anyhow because the New Gaffer was saying something about how we must all be there to accept the shared responsibility of the situation we find ourselves in, and the atmosphere afterwards was absolute magic. We was all singing and dancing and having a right laugh on the coach back. At one point, I looked down the aisle at Wattsy and Vic and Bob and that lot, all leaping about on the back seat and flashing V-signs and mooning at any cars we pass what's full of rival fans and I'm suddenly overcome with it all. These are my lads, my muckers. It's hard to explain, but it's like having another family, being in a professional football team. You live together, you work together, you go out together, oh aye and you'd die for each other out there on the park. I look at them and I feel this lump rising in me throat. I realise it would be madness to leave them. Kenny Dalglish could offer us a long 'un a day and I'd still prefer to be here, where I belong, among lads I belong with.

There and then I decide that's it, I'll stay and fight for my place. Get back in there where I should be. Because this is my home and these are my people.

My train of thought is only partly disturbed by Donald ringing on the mobile with news of me other home. The house.

'There's a problem with the drains, lad,' he says. 'Terrible stench throughout. So bad some of the lads have downed tools.'

I tell him, get bleedin' Dynorod round and get on with it. Jesus knob, some people's lives are so pathetic.

Thursday 30th

I'm on the physio's table, having me stiffness attended to by the lovely Suzette, when Old Demo comes marching in and tells me to get out there. I'm needed as a marker to give the new YTS kid sensation some practice before Saturday's game.

'I've put Wattsy on him yesterday and the lad's lost a bit of confidence,' says Demo. 'I want to build his morale back up, so I needs you out there.'

Well, I've told the old codger straight off that Darren Tackle is in no way, shape or form fit for combat of any sort. I've told him, with the World Cup ahead, I need to conserve my energy, not get out there and get me shins kicked to pieces in some poxy training-ground exercise.

'World Cup?' he says. 'You going to the World Cup? Who with, the St John's Ambulance Brigade?'

Mock ye not, Demo. It's true. Out the blue I got a call on the mobile yesterday from, believe it or not, that wassock Tristram or whatever he's called. He says I've been picked for one of the most important, prestigious squads going out to France '98. That's right, the Three Lions corporate hospitality team. It's a tough assignment, involving wining and dining punters who have paid £2,000 a throw for a ticket retailing at £27.50. I'm contracted to be there minimum for every England group match. Plus an option for beyond, if we qualify. Obviously, like every true Englishman, I hope we'll go all the way to the final, if only because the fee is a long 'un a game plus two match tickets. Imagine the return you'll get flogging a pair for the final on to the lads in the camel-coloured coats.

As it happens, I wasn't the first celeb they was after. According to that Tristram they wanted all the lads what appear in the World Cup merchandise, then never made the cut for the real squad. You know the ones, the geezers like Coley and Hinchcliffey and Gazza who've got their mug on the Sainsbury's coin collection and the BP cigarette cards, but, like Darren Tackle himself, by some oversight were not picked for the actual squad by His Glenness. But them lot's fees are too high. So apparently the Three Lions lot was looking instead for someone in the next category down. But since all Rodders' other clients were still all too pricey for them, that Tristram thought of me.

'Please do it, Mr T,' he says. 'I'm on a commission for every celeb I sign and I've not landed one yet. You were the only person I could think of desperate enough to do it. Oh do say yes, Mr T, do.'

All right by me, it's nice to be part of it. Besides, all cash is good cash as far as yours truly is concerned. My role out there is to mix with other tip-top celebs – no one else as yet confirmed, but that Tristram's still negotiating with Rory McGrath, Nobby Stiles and that wassock from *Fantasy Football* what wears a dressing-gown. We'll be schmoozing the fans, providing added value, making the punters laugh, telling them insider yarns. Trying, basically, to get them so pissed they don't notice how much they're paying. In order to do that, you have to be at the absolute peak of mental form. And frankly, the last thing I needs right now with an important assignment like that looming is to go out there and play football.

MAY

Saturday 2nd

YTS kid scores again to give us three more points. The maths is now certain: provided everyone else loses next Sunday, we only need a point to stay in the big time. Well, I says we. Darren Tackle's contribution to the latest rescue bid was to be sat in the Alliance & Leicester Stand surrounded by nonces singing the theme to *The Great Escape*. Needless to say, I didn't join in. My mood was not exactly enhanced by being approached outside the ground by a geezer with a microphone from the local radio asking for a supporter's reaction to the Greens' plight.

'Do you not know who I am?' I says.

He looks me up and down (handy new Hugo Boss suit I'm wearing what I bought for the World Cup gig, so in all honesty there shouldn't have been any mistaking) and he says: 'Oh, sorry mate. You're supporting the opposition, aren't you?'

Tuesday 5th

Donald bells us on the mobile as I'm lying on the massage table being pummelled by the lovely Suzette to tell us that Dynorod had been yesterday, spent all afternoon cleaning out the drains, the bill was £768.35 but the house still stinks. In fact all the lads had downed tools and I couldn't expect to see a finish on the work until September at the earliest.

'Donald,' I says, floating off on a Suzette-inspired haze of relaxation and contentment, 'you're mistaking me for someone who gives a shit.'

Wednesday 6th

Hey, don't get me wrong. As a professional I am 100 per cent committed to this club. As far as the Greens go I very much give a shit. And with the all-roughage diet I'm still on I give one regular and all.

What I meant was, right now is the time for minds to focus on the job in hand and not be distracted by domestics. Now is the time to leave your private life on the doorstep, as Rodders used to say.

Focus is everything. We have got to do it this weekend: for the New Gaffer, who's stood by us all since he's been here; for the supporters what pay good money to see us and who are entitled to expect better; but most of all, for ourselves. It's our professional pride what's at stake here.

That sound all right? Just practising should Mr Chairman's fly-on-the-wall documentary team want a comment from yours truly during the course of the week. As yet no one's asked us. But best be prepared.

Friday 8th

They say that a condemned man's last day passes in a flash. And I kind of see what they mean. Not that waiting to be hung or popped on the electric chair can be worse than the torment we are suffering. Our very Premiership lives are on the line. Yet it only seems like yesterday that the season started, with all that optimism and excitement and cheering and expectation. Though why we had all that after a 0–0 draw with Coventry is anyone's guess.

Now here we are on the brink of the end, with all our questions shortly to be answered. Will it be Premiership or Nationwide? Death or glory? And more particularly, will I have tempted fate by wearing me lucky cream Armani suit as modelled on the one the Liverpool hombres wore at the Cup Final in '96?

One thing's for sure, this last game of the season has certainly caught the imagination of the town. Everywhere I've gone, everyone's asked me the same question: 'Hoy, Dazz, got any spares?' Me mobile has not stopped ringing with people I haven't spoken to for ten years getting all friendly. Even mam give us a bell yesterday.

'You couldn't do us sixteen together could you, Darren?'

'Mam,' I says. 'What you want with sixteen together?'

In fact, she doesn't need one together. She hasn't been to see me play for ten years, ever since I got sent off for the youth team and she said she was so ashamed that she'd never come back. Apparently me shorts were filthy and she thought everyone was looking at her for letting me out of the house in dirty snags.

'They're for our Clayton,' she says.

'But he's never been to see me either,' I says.

'I know, love, but some of his friends down the Ferry want to come.'

'I never knew them lot was keen,' I says.

'Oh yes, love. I heard him on the phone telling someone he could get any number of tickets through you. Fella told him he wanted sixteen, and you know what our Clayton's like, he was thrilled just to be able to help him. He said if I could get him the tickets through you, he'd clean up. Which is good of him as his room is a bit of a mess.'

Saturday 9th

Tomorrow it is then. Knob it. I've just got this feeling in me stomach that we've had it. And the really worrying thing is: Darren Tackle's hunches are never wrong.

Sunday 10th

We've done it. Survived like I always knew we would. Yes! Result!

Mind you, there was a close call. Too close for comfort. I'm sweating just thinking about it.

It happened after we'd scraped the point we needed with a last-minute equaliser. True, the oppo had three goals disallowed and four men sent off, one for making his own way to the touchline to change his shorts when he should have gone on the stretcher. And we only managed to put the ball in the net when Darko scored at the third attempt from a disputed penalty. But over a long season these things tend to even themselves out. And I'm pretty delighted to have played my role: last five minutes on for Wattsy. Demo sent us on, saying it might be my last chance for a kick for the Greens. Didn't get one as it happens, but at least I was in on the celebrations. And what celebrations. Whole Daihatsu went mental: I saw grown men crying. Though admittedly the grown man I saw crying was the catering manager blubbing about how now we're staying in the Premiership that means the Liverpool scallies will still be coming down again next year thieving all his meat and potato pies in the away end.

Anyhow, back to the close call. There's one hell of a party in the dressing-room after the game and in comes the Sky mob looking for interviews and that, so Vic and Bob done the honours and chucked George Gavin in the bath. And there I was sitting naked, when the camera comes spinning over. It could've been well embarrassing, if I hadn't have been dead handy with a towel. See, I was drinking a can of Carling – they drop a few cases in the dressing-room as part of the sponsorship deal with the Premiership – and luckily I sees the camera out the corner of my eye and just manage to slip it under the towel in time. Doh. Imagine: caught supping Carling. Coolness rating down into the sauna zone.

Monday 11th

It's all beginning to sink in. The atmosphere, the match, the result. How we done it, I'll never know. It was a bleedin' tense afternoon all round. And there seemed to be several people who should have known better what seemed to be doing their best to make it even tenser.

Take the New Gaffer. We're 1–0 down at half-time, not had a shot on target, playing like a bunch of no-hope nonces, Nationwide about to welcome us with open arms and what does he do? He remains calm. I mean, what kind of Gaffer is that? Where was the rollicking? Where was the threats, the screams, the physical violence? How does he expect a team of modern-day professionals to go out there and perform without a single expletive ringing in their ears? I wasn't the only one who noticed. The goateed wassock from Mr Chairman's fly-on-the-wall documentary looked like he'd just lost the winning lottery ticket at the end of the New Gaffer's half-time talk.

'Not good television,' I heard him tell the cameraman as we went back out.

And talking of Mr Chairman, he's another one what didn't help. First off, to protect himself, geezer orders the biggest peace-time security operation this side of the one Bill Clinton gets when he goes out for a bit of bird-watching in Washington of a Friday night. Says he's worried that if we go down in the last match, the students what run the fanzines will get all uppity and start chucking bricks through the windows of his executive boxes. Fella says he's genuinely worried for the safety of the well-heeled.

I mean, what kind of message does that send down to the lads in the dressing-room just as they is preparing for the biggest game of their lives? Sorry, lads, the geezer what owns the club hasn't got any faith in you lot to do the necessary and actually win, so he's hired in half the Metropolitan police force, backed up by a bunch of mercenaries what have just come back from Sierra Leone, to cover his back.

Then, to compound it all, when us lads put on the performance of the season, do our bit and save the geezer's hide, he only goes and blabs to the hyenas at the press conference about how he's going to be opening the chequebook over the summer and buy in the talent necessary to stop this sort of thing happening next year.

'Rest assured,' he told Motty on the *Match of the Day* special. 'You know me, tell it how it is. I guarantee we will not be in this position come twelve months. I will have bought in the players to ensure we don't. And some of the familiar faces who let us down this year will not be around come kick-off next season.'

So thanks a bunch, Mr Chairman. We put our shins on the line to maintain the value of your share price, then you tell us we'll all be surplus to requirements once you've schmoozed Johnny Foreigner to come over and pick up his pound of flesh in the Daihatsu next season. Well, Darren Tackle for one is not going to put up with that sort of malarkey. He'll be fighting every inch of the way for his place in the team next season. To be back there with Wattsy, Vic, Bob and Darko: the lads what care for this club. Who are this club. The lads what done it for you.

One other thing. I remember afterwards, after the dressing-room party's died down and George Gavin's dried off his suit and we've all agreed to meet up at Wattsy's for laters, I'm on my way out into the match-day car-park under the Alliance & Leicester and I can hear all the nonces dancing and celebrating outside like we'd just won summat, and I'm sure I seen the ref leaning out his car window and being handed an envelope by Mr Chairman and then driving off like he's being chased by Dennis Wise looking for a cab. I says to Mr Chairman when I catch up with him, who's that you was talking to.

He says: 'Dunno, Darren, but it wasn't the ref. Definitely not. You know me, what's on me lung's on me tongue, tell it how it is, say what's there to be said. And it wasn't the ref. No, no, no.'

I could've sworn it was. Must've been that Carling.

Tuesday 12th

People talk about too much football that your modern pro has to play, but what about too much holiday? Two days into the break and already I'm bored. There's another five weeks of this before me little World Cup jaunt, stretching out endlessly ahead, with nothing to do but lie around mam's house checking Ceefax every five minutes to see if anyone's put a bid in for yours truly. As yet not a flicker.

Your ordinary punter, though, with your ordinary job – you know, like ringing people up at night trying to flog dodgy kitchens – they've got no clue how tedious this is. I envy them what only have two weeks on the bounce. Honest, I do. Anyhow, here's a list of ways I've thought up of filling my time:

1. Get bladdered.
2. Can't think of anything else.

Thursday 14th

Summat to do tonight, all right. Mr Chairman's fly-on-the-wall documentary is being screened. Was to go out in the autumn, apparently, but they had to rush it out for legal reasons. Sounds fruity.

To be honest, as I'm watching, I'm a little bit disappointed. I mean, there's footage of Mr Chairman's meet with a *feng shui* expert telling him where to place his desk in his new lottery-funded office suite down at the training ground (with a special position for Thursday nights, no doubt). The camera's in on a meet of the marketing people talking about the need to maximise merchandise growth differentials by producing a limited-edition shirt for reserve team aways. And there's the catering manager revealing that his losses this season were largely down to the introduction of scampi to the outlet in the River Street End, what had only sold three portions all year.

'That's a hell of a waste of seafood every Saturday,' he says.

There's even footage of that Tristram or whatever he's called getting into his Fi-Fi the Flounder costume and trying to get the crowd to get involved for a bleedin' change.

'I see myself as an artiste,' Fif-Fi tells the goatee. 'And the Daihatsu is my stage.'

Funny that, most people sees you as a twat.

Basically, I accept, these is all-important parts of running your modern-day Premiership football club these days. But are they the ones anyone's interested in?

You see, frankly, though there's endless amounts of the goateed wassock asking his stupid questions ('What,' he asks Wattsy at one point, 'is the principal concrete aesthetic of the sliding tackle?'), I reckon the film's major drawback is this: there's not enough appearances by yours truly. I've only been on screen three times so far, twice in the background and once in that one-on-one interview where I'm telling the goateed wassock quite forcefully how I should be in the team, how I'm better than Wattsy and Vic and Bob and all of them, how the New Gaffer hasn't got a clue and how things had better start changing pronto around the Daihatsu if Darren Tackle's name is to be associated with the place next season.

So that's what I think of the programme: not enough of what makes the Greens the Greens, i.e. me.

That is, until the final sequence, the one after the credits have rolled, which, I have to say, takes us a bit by surprise as I'm sitting there on mam's sofa, the sound up to maximum to drown out the blubbin' from Hayley and her brat.

The camera zooms in on Bob (in the absence of yours truly, something of the programme's star so far with his endless practical jokes) who is inside some sort of building site. It's not absolutely clear what's happening, because it's night time, but you can just make out that he's not alone. There's Vic next to him as usual, and there's Wattsy and Darko and Hermann lurking in the background for deffo. I'm pretty sure I spots Gary Ball and Mickey Scanlan and all. And isn't that the YTS kid? We're talking basically most of the lads. Though not me. I must have been out injured or summat.

Anyhow, Bob has these plastic bags filled with his usual comic material and he's putting them under the floorboards of this room what's obviously just being built. I'm trying to work out where it is, and I'm thinking it must be Mr Chairman's new office suite, when you can hear the voice of the goateed wassock off-camera.

'So what exactly is the purpose of this particular exercise?'

'We want to show the tool once and for all,' Bob says, and I'm thinking it's got to be Mr Chairman's gaff, for deffo. 'We're sick of him with his whingeing and his whining and his thinking he's Jack the lad. It's not as if he's any good. He's shite. And we've all had enough of him.'

'So it's a sort of excretal critical statement,' you hear the goateed voice say.

'Dunno about that,' says Bob, shovelling the bags under the floorboards. 'Funny thing is, it's his own shite. He collected it for me.'

You what?

'Oh I see,' says goatee. 'So, as it were, in a sense, Darren Tackle is being hoist by his own discharge.'

'Yeah, shit shall return to the shit,' says Bob. 'It's biblical, innit.'

Knob, I recognise that place now: it's my gaff. That's

what Donald's bleedin' stench was. That's what Bob's
ultimate turd-joke was. That's what's been going on. I've
been stitched up big-style. Darren Tackle, kippered up like
a twat on national television.

'What the gentlemen of the Greens are saying is this,'
says Wattsy, leaning right into the camera, eyes wide
with that look he gets when he's just about to take out
an opposing forward at cruciate height. 'Darren Tackle:
you're shit and you know you are.'

Christ.

Then it just dawns on me. Slowly and painfully.

Nobody likes me.

POSTSCRIPT

JUNE

Friday 12th

The fall-out from Mr Chairman's fly-on-the-wall documentary mings on. For three weeks, the papers is full of nothing else. So mam tells us. I've not had the heart to read them meself.

The FA have got involved, the PFA, UEFA, FIFA. I'm surprised the RSPCA haven't put their oar in over the issue of cruelty to the Dog. The New Gaffer resigned in protest, Mr Chairman tried to sue the BBC and the goateed wassock had to leave the country, as anyone of Green persuasion has made it clear they'd take his head off if they ever ran into him. The only person what emerged with dignity intact is Fi-Fi the Flounder.

As for me, well I've just stayed indoors at mam's house, trying to keep out the way of the hyenas camped outside and waiting for the phone to ring with an offer from another club. Trouble is, no one can get through what with the hyenas blocking the line with their endless requests for a quote. But what can I say to them? Except yes, the bags are all still there under the floorboards because Donald won't soil his hands and actually remove them.

Monday 15th

I'm out the house for the first time in a month today. Off on that World Cup gig with the corporate hospitality mob: day trip to Marseille. I've got to be at Luton for a 5.30 a.m. plane and Claudia from Three Lions, my contact, tells us they'll be sending a limo to get me there, arriving at 2.00 a.m. and don't forget me passport.

I should have smelt a nause about Three Lions straight off. The 'limo' arrives at 3.15 and is, in fact, a D-reg Nissan Cherry driven by a geezer what announces that he's a life-long Blue and we Green bastards deserve everything we get, and he's not had such a laugh as that documentary since Man U. went down in 1974. If I'd've thought of it I'd've left a Bob-style tip under his back seat, but unfortunately I didn't think about it until about four hours later.

Not that I didn't have plenty of time for thinking. Two hours, in fact, spent waiting for the Three Lions charter flight to take off from Luton. Two hours spent listening to a bunch of pin-striped wassocks endlessly whingeing to Claudia (handy piece, as it happens) about the booze running out on the plane and how they'd paid two long 'uns a head to rub shoulders with celebrities and all they've got is some geezer what once refereed the Welsh Cup final, a regional heat winner of *Mastermind* and – and I quote – 'that sad loser Darren Tackle'.

So me and me clients are not exactly off on a tip-top footing.

I tell you, after two hours of listening to a bunch of braying pin-stripes barking like seals and chanting 'we want champagne' I take back all I said about the unwashed in the River Street End. I accept it's all right for the corporate hospitality sector to behave like this because they've paid more for this trip than the average working man makes in two months. But I can't really see why they're any different to our Lee and our Clayton, who, when they used to go abroad with the lads from the Baby-Faced Stanley Firm and have a few, was generally considered a national disgrace. I says to one of the pinstripes who's just chundered over the back of the referee geezer, what's the difference between him and his mates and the hoolies?

'Here's the difference, loser. They get drunk on the scum's drink, beer. We get drunk on the top people's drink, champagne. It's post-modern, it's clever. It's irony, you see. We are the irony generation. Which reminds me,' he says, looking towards that Claudia, 'where's the champagne, bitch?'

Eventually we gets to Marseille, though no thanks to the plane, what looks like it's powered by a rubber band, and the pin-stripes who start throwing their weight around in passport control winding up the Froggie officials so much, two of them get strip-searched. As a result we miss the champagne reception overlooking the harbour, as promised in the Three Lions itinerary.

Just as well, I reckon, as I want to spend as little time as possible in the company of this lot, but the pin-stripes start braying to such a degree that Claudia stops the minibus outside a shop and stacks up on a case of the bubbly stuff. Sweetheart and all, she remembers to buy me a six-pack of lager, which slips down a treat till I reads the label and discovers it's Tunisian.

We gets to the ground with no more than ten minutes to kick-off and it's like a bleedin' military operation to get anywhere near the turnstiles. There's geezers checking us for booze, checking us for weapons, blokes looking at our tickets. Every check-point I go through, some bloke stops me and has a word into his walkie-talkie. I'm getting well naused by the whole thing, though to be fair I got a bit of a result getting separated from the pin-stripes in the endless queue.

I'm just about to get through the last nause-up and I can hear the crowd inside getting well warmed up and I'm beginning at last to think maybe this was all worthwhile, when yet another bleedin' official – all blazered up and carrying a clipboard – takes us to one side and asks for me ticket, me passport, me plane ticket, the works. After he's inspected one against the other about four times, and spoken to a couple of geezers on his walkie-talkie and bascially behaved like he's leading the worldwide fight against international organised crime instead of being some tosser jobsworth of a turnstile operator, he eventually drops his little bombshell.

'I'm afraid I can't let you in, sir.'

'Eh?' I says. 'There must be some mistake.'

'No mistake,' he says. 'You're not coming in.'

'Is it me ticket?' I says, nice and slow and loud, since he's foreign and that. 'Cos I got that off-of them Three Lions, I'm working for them lot. Celeb hospitality and all that. Am I making myself understood?'

'Nothing wrong with your ticket, sir.'

My flabber is that gasted, I go straight for the big one, even though usually I try to reserve it only for emergencies. Bringing meself to me full height, I says: 'Do you know who I am?'

'Yes I do,' says this Frog. 'You're Darren Tackle.'

'Exactly,' I says. 'So you've got to let us in.'

'No, you don't understand,' says Froggie. 'It's because you are Darren Tackle that you are not coming in.'

I says: 'You what?'

'Let me put this in words of less than three syllables,' he says, beginning to get a bit shirty. 'You Darren Tackle. You not coming in. *Capisce*?'

'You seem to speak pretty handy English for a Frog,' I says.

'That's because I am English,' he says. 'I'm from the Football Intelligence Unit helping the French Interior Ministry to wheedle out potential trouble-makers.'

'Well, thank God for that,' I says. 'So you'll know that

there must've been a mistake. I mean you are on our side, incha? Bulldog spirit? British invasion? Hop off you Frogs and that?'

'No mistake, sir,' he says. 'The rules are quite clear: no supporter with a conviction for assault is being allowed in.'

'Well, there you go, see,' I says. 'I'm not a supporter, I'm a pro.'

'We have to be seen to be even-handed, sir. Player or supporter, anyone with a conviction for assault will be turned away.'

'Conviction for assault? But I ain't got a . . .'

Oh knob. Not that again. Three years ago, outside a bar down River Street, I chinned a geezer for trying to get involved after I'd given LeeAnne a little warning slap. I was out for a month with broken knuckles, got a six-month suspended at the mags' court and a monster fine from the Boss. Now I can't get in the knobbin' World Cup. I can't believe it. I am being denied entry to the most crucial international of my lifetime because some busybody wants to stick their nose in a touch of domestics. I blame the media and that, constantly trying to pry into footballers' private lives.

'Now please, sir,' says the geezer. 'If you'll clear the way and allow the *bona fide* fans in, it would be appreciated.'

'What you on about?' I says, as he eases me out the queue. 'I'll have your badge number! This could be the end of your career! You're stuffed, mate! I'll have you!'

I'm still screaming abuse as I'm led off in an arm-lock by two local cops: Frog-marched I suppose you'd have to call it. If only Wattsy had been here. He has a way with dibble. He'd have sorted them, Wattsy. Or Rodders. He'd have fixed it. Or Donald. He'd have knocked a hole in the perimeter fence to see me through.

Instead, I'm on me own, separated from the wassocks

wanting hospitality, with Claudia from Three Lions nowhere to be seen, being taken outside the total exclusion zone set up round the ground to keep the hoolies at bay. Ten minutes' forced march later, the cops leave me to me fate in downtown Marseille, surrounded by a right lairy bunch of locals eyeing me up and down as I stand there in me Hugo Boss.

I'm just brushing down me dignity when I spots a bar over the road. So I thinks: sod it. Do what the rest of the country'll be doing: watch the match on telly, have a few. I've just sat at the table, waiting for a waiter, when the mobile rings.

'That Dazz?' says this voice.

'Depends who wants to know,' I says.

'Dazz, it's me.'

'Who?' I says.

'Fuckenell, eh? Eh? Forgotten all fucken ready?'

'Boss?' I says, almost jumping out the seat, before remembering me previous in the mobile wind-up department. 'Oh aye, very clever Wattsy.'

'Fuckenell son, what the fuckenell are you on about?'

I have to take me hat off to the geezer, he's getting better that Wattsy, sounds just like the Boss.

'I'd've thought you'd've had enough with all the Bob shit, Wattsy. Leave us alone, eh,' I says.

'Bob shit? What the fuckenell you on about, son? This is the Boss.'

'You sure?' I says.

'Fuckenell, I should know who the fuckenell I is, son.'

Knob. It is him.

'Sorry, Boss, just my little joke,' I says. 'Where are you?'

'In Lyon,' he says. 'Looking at Iran versus fucken America. Hoping to pick up a few Ayatollahs on the cheap.'

'Who for, Boss?'

'Don't you read the papers, son?' he says. And to be honest, I have been a bit detached in the news department these last few weeks. 'I'm taking over the Blues next season, son. That's why I'm ringing. I want you there. Build the team around you. Get Darren Tackle back out on the park where he belongs.'

Knob. The Blues. I've been dying for an out this past month, looking anywhere for a signing-on fee. You know, an offer from Newcastle, Arsenal, Spurs, somewhere like that. And instead a lifeline comes in from them bastards. I've been a Green all me life, ever since me and our Clayton and our Lee used to jib into the Alliance & Leicester when it was just known as the Morley Street East terracing. I've been with them through thick and thin – well, thin and thinner. Cut me and I'd bleed green. Specially after a night on the crème de menthe. Now, all of a sudden, here they are expecting me to turn out for them blue twats. It can't be done. No way. Every man has his pride. And Darren Tackle has more than most.

'Not the Blues, Boss,' I says. 'You know me, Green through and through.'

'Tell you what I'm offering, Dazz,' says the Boss. 'Twelve long 'uns a week, plus a Klinsmann, can't say fairer than that.'

'A Klinsmann?' I says. 'You're joking.'

'No, straight up. You're on a Jurgen the moment you sign up, son.'

A Klinsmann: every pro's dream, a clause in your contract stating you can never be dropped, never be separated from the comfort zone of them win bonuses, never be left on the bench with the prying eye of the Sky camera up your nostrils and Andy Gray speculating about your comeback chances. A Klinsmann. Sod it. It may be the Blues, but you'd have to be a half-wit to turn down a Klinsmann.

'Sorted,' I says.

'Fuckenell, eh?' says the Boss. 'I'm fucken made up. The old partnership, back in the old fucken routine. Wait till I tell me Chairman. See you in pre-season.'

Top or what? I'm just about to call the waiter over to order a little celebratory lager or two when the mobile goes again.

'A'right, boy,' says this voice.

'Rodders?' I says.

'Right first time, boy. Listen, I've heard on the grapevine, little dickey tells me, that you've been having a little wossname, a chat with the old Boss. About joining the Blues. Am I right?'

'Depends, Rods,' I says.

'Don't let the bleeders rip you off, boy. What you needs is an agent to negotiate for you.'

'Yeah, well, I haven't got an agent,' I says.

'Wrong,' he says.

'What agent would want me, Rods?' I says.

'You're talkin' to him, boy.'

'Who?'

'Me, boy.'

'Straight up, Rods, you'll have me back?'

'That's what I'm saying, boy. That's basically it in a nutshell. From my mouth to God's ear, not a word of a lie. We'll chat later, boy. Right now I'm busy, got some eggs to boil. Bell me. Speakcha.'

Yesss! Darren Tackle is back. After all the trials, the tribulations, the nausing and the bollocks of this season, a true pro shows his colours. He is back, back, back. Backer than Burt Bacharach on a comeback tour. There's only one thing for it: get bladdered.

'Oi, garlic breath,' I shouts to the waiter. 'Dos lagers, por favor. And make it snappy.'

'I'm sorry, sir,' says the waiter. 'Police rules. No alcohol can be served within a 25-kilometre radius of a football ground during an England match. If sir would prefer, I can get you a mineral water like the footballers drink.'

Oh knob.

Somehow that sums up my season.